Tasting Harmony

Eb Edition

by Greg Fishman

Published by Greg Fishman Jazz Studios
Evanston, Illinois 60202

ISBN: 0-9766153-9-2

Published by Greg Fishman Jazz Studios
824 Custer Avenue, Evanston, Illinois 60202
www.gregfishmanjazzstudios.com
e-mail: greg@gregfishmanjazzstudios.com

Tasting Harmony
Table of Contents

PREFACE

Tasting Harmony is a new approach to ear training, utilizing the concept of synesthesia, the mixing of the senses. A common form of synesthesia in relation to music occurs when someone hears a sound and sees or imagines a color associated with that particular sound. I've found that it is also possible to mix the sense of taste with the sense of sound.

Tasting Harmony taps into the ability we all possess to discern the flavors of food items and uses that ability to recognize the sounds of notes in a wide variety of chords.

If I mention food items such as bananas, carrots, chocolate cake, pizza, etc., you can vividly recall the flavor, temperature, texture, color and taste of each food item. For example, you would never confuse the taste of pizza with the taste of a banana. Each has a unique flavor and character.

Now, imagine that instead of describing food items, I'm describing the sound of a particular note over a chord: a flatted ninth played with a dominant seventh chord, or a sharp eleventh played with a major seventh chord. Each note has a unique flavor and character, both of which can change in an instant, depending on the type of chord being played, and the placement of the note within the chord. It is this "flavor" that I "listen" for when I'm playing.

Just as we all have our favorite "comfort foods," we can have "comfort sounds" which are also familiar favorites. *Tasting Harmony* helps establish an emotional connection to your note choices by providing you with a harmonic menu of eighty-one different sounds played in all twelve keys...that's nine hundred and seventy-two chords you'll hear and "taste" with each listening to the play-along CD.

The chord progression of every song represents a harmonic recipe created by the composer. *Tasting Harmony* allows you to fully stock your ear with the ingredients needed for each recipe, so you don't have to substitute water for cream when it's time to put those ingredients together to bake your harmonic creation.

Sing and play along with vocalist Petra van Nuis and pianist Jeremy Kahn as they take you through a full menu of ear-enriching harmonic flavors.

Tasting Harmony was developed to provide a fun approach for all musicians who want to get involved with harmony on a deeper level in a direct and non-theoretical way. I hope that you get many years of enjoyment from this book. It has been my privilege to write it for you.

— Greg Fishman

PERSONNEL CREDITS

Petra van Nuis – Vocals, spoken announcements and cover model

Petra van Nuis is a featured vocalist and recording artist on the Chicago jazz scene where she sings regularly at such prominent venues as the Jazz Showcase, the Green Mill, and Andy's Jazz Club with such renowned musicians as Judy Roberts, Andy Brown, Art Davis, Russ Phillips, Greg Fishman, and Jeremy Kahn. Petra has performed at numerous jazz festivals, including the prestigious Chautauqua Jazz Party and the Tribute to Bix Fest. She has played clubs around the country including Firefly Jazz Club (Ann Arbor, MI), Terra Blues (NYC), Ear Inn (NYC), Swing 46 (NYC), Night Town (Cleveland), and the Blue Wisp Jazz Club (Cincinnati, OH). Internationally, she has played the Gorinchem Jazz Festival in Holland, and Antwerp's top jazz club, the Jazz Hopper. Whenever she sings, in concert or on CD, Petra's fresh, appealing voice and unique sound always connect with people.

Jeremy Kahn – Piano

Jeremy Kahn is one of Chicago's most versatile pianists, playing in jazz venues, orchestra pits and concert halls from New York to Rotterdam to Singapore. He has performed with such musical giants as Dizzy Gillespie, Max Roach, Aretha Franklin, Phil Woods, Ray Brown, Charlie Haden, Joni Mitchell, Gal Costa, Joe Williams, Chris Potter, and Helen Merrill to name but a few. He is a graduate of the New England Conservatory of Music, and has been a guest on Marian McPartland's NPR radio show, "Piano Jazz." He has played in the orchestra for many Broadway shows, including "The Lion King," and "Wicked." Jeremy has performed extensively in Chicago's top jazz clubs and jazz fests, and is famous for his ability to brilliantly and authentically cover all styles of jazz piano.

PRODUCTION CREDITS

Written by: Greg Fishman
Published by: Greg Fishman Jazz Studios, Evanston, Illinois
Edited by: Judy Roberts
Cover Model: Petra van Nuis
Photography and graphic design by: Bogdon Nastase, Chicago, Illinois
Book printing: Omnigraphix, Morton Grove, Illinois
CD Printing: Universal Recording Supplies, Inc., Lakewood, New Jersey
Music engraving: Greg Fishman
CD Recorded at Studiomedia, Evanston, Illinois
Engineered, mixed and mastered by Scott Steinman

SUGGESTED USE OF THIS BOOK AND CD SET

HARMONIC CONTEXT

One of the most important things to learn as a musician is the indispensable skill of singing (or playing) one note while listening to the other notes being sung (or played) by the other musicians in your group.

Tasting Harmony is designed to teach your ear to focus on the sound of each individual chord tone while simultaneously hearing the full chord. The piano accompaniment on the play-along CD provides the harmonic context for every chord tone, from the root to the thirteenth, played as a part of eleven different types of chords. After working with the CD, you'll internalize the sounds of the chords being played by the pianist on the recording and will start to develop the ability to hear the full sounds of the chords in your mind, even when you play individual notes in the cycle with no accompaniment. Hearing in this manner is not something you can simply decide to do. It's something that will naturally occur once you've spent enough time training your ear to hear notes in a variety of harmonic contexts. In order to hear "in context" you need to develop the ability to hear notes in addition to the individual note you're singing or playing.

In order to hear in this manner, you need to have a clear memory of a particular sound or "flavor." Let's use a food analogy to help clarify this concept. What if I asked you to recall the taste and texture of fresh strawberries, but you'd never eaten a strawberry in your life? You would not be able to imagine the taste because recalling it would require that you've experienced the taste for yourself. Just as there's no way to guess at how a strawberry tastes, there's no way to guess the sound of a particular chord. You need to "taste" and experience the sound of chord first, and *then* you can recall it.

Let's examine another food analogy. Imagine the taste of a juicy piece of pineapple. Do you have the flavor of the pineapple in your mind? Now, quickly, imagine the taste of that pineapple on a slice of pizza! You might say "yuck, pineapple on pizza," or "yum, Hawaiian style pizza," but I'll bet that it evoked some kind of gut-level response of what it would taste like, right? This is the same way that I can imagine combining sounds in my mind, so that by the time I pick up my horn, I'm very clear on the individual pitches (pineapples) and the chords (pizza) upon which they're placed.

CHORD FAMILIES

I've included eighty-one different harmonic contexts for notes over the most popular chords used in modern jazz. To keep things well organized, I've grouped the chord types into eleven "families" as follows:

1. Major 7th chords
2. Dominant 7th chords (with major 9ths)
3. Dominant 7th sus chords
4. Dominant 7th chords (with flat 9ths)
5. Dominant 7th chords (with sharp 9ths)
6. Minor 7th chords
7. Minor with Major 7th chords
8. Minor 7b5 chords (half-diminished chords)
9. Diminished 7th chords
10. Major 6th chords
11. Minor 6th chords

In regard to the order in which the chord families appear, I've arranged the first nine chord families from very "sweet" (major seventh chords) to very "tart" (diminished seventh chords). I've placed the major and minor sixth chords (tenth and eleventh families) last because their intervallic structure is different from the first nine chord families.

THE CIRCLE OF FOURTHS (CYCLE OF FIFTHS)

The circle of fourths (also known as the cycle of fifths, and sometimes simply as "the cycle") is the most common of all chord progressions. I think of this sequence of notes as a sort of harmonic gravity, in that there is a natural "pull" towards the next note in the cycle. All jazz musicians need to memorize and master this sequence of notes.

Practice singing the cycle (C, F, Bb, Eb, Ab, Db, Gb, B, E, A, D and G) a cappella. Next, play the cycle on your instrument. For this Eb edition of *Tasting Harmony,* the cycle always starts on a written G (concert Bb). This means that for one complete "round" of the cycle, you would sing (or play): G, C, F, Bb, Eb, Ab, Db, Gb, B, E, A and D.

Chord progressions using the cycle often involve different chord types, such as the ii7 / V7 / IMaj7 progression (Dmi7 / G7 / CMaj7). However, for ease of use and harmonic consistency, this first volume of *Tasting Harmony* uses just one chord type per track played through the cycle.

CONSISTENT STARTING NOTE (Bb Concert)

A unique feature of this book is that the first note of every track starts on a concert Bb. For example, with track one, Petra sings the roots of major seventh chords, starting with BbMaj7. On track two, Petra sings thirds on major seventh chords. Again, she starts the track by singing a Bb concert. Since the Bb is now acting as the third of the chord, the pianist transposes the chords, starting the cycle on a GbMaj7 chord. On track three, Petra sings Bb once more, and this time, the Bb is acting as the fifth of the chord. The pianist now starts the chord progression with an EbMaj7 chord.

This pattern continues throughout each of the chord families, with Petra singing the cycle starting (and ending) on a concert Bb while the pianist transposes the chord progression. This was done for two reasons. First, it keeps the notes in an easy register for both men and women to sing with ease and comfort. (Men will usually sing an octave below Petra). Secondly, it allows the student to experience the different flavor of the Bb when it's acting as the root versus the third, fifth, seventh, ninth, etc.

USING THE CD

Petra announces the degree of the chord as well as the chord type and then sings the notes in the circle of fourths. All tracks start with concert Bb and go through the cycle one time until arriving back "home" at concert Bb. The CD can also be used without this book for training your ear while commuting, walking, working out, etc.

CD TRACK LISTINGS

The table below lists each chord tone for all of the chords on the play-along CD. I recommend using the CD in the original order of tracks for most ear training situations. However, if you'd like to train for a specific pitch, use the chart below to determine which tracks are needed to achieve your goals. For example, if you wanted to work with the thirds of every chord family, you would program your CD player to play tracks: 2, 10, 18, 26, 35, 44, 51, 58, 65, 73 and 78.

A note about the asterisks (*) used in the chart: There were two cases (the sharp fifth on major sevenths and the flat ninth on suspended dominants) in which I felt that it was more aesthetically pleasing and helpful to the listener to have the chords presented in a slightly different order.

CHORD FAMILY	ROOT	3rd	5TH	#5TH	6th	7TH	b9th	9th	#9th	11th	#11th	13th
Major 7th	1	2	3	8*		4		5			6	7
Dominant 7th	9	10	11	12		13		14			15	16
Dominant 7th sus	17	18	19			20	22*	21		23		24
Dominant 7th b9	25	26	27	28		29	30		31		32	33
Dominant 7th #9	34	35	36	37		38	39		40		41	42
Minor 7th	43	44	45			46		47		48		49
Minor w/Major 7th	50	51	52			53		54		55		56
Minor 7b5	57	58	59			60		61		62		63
Diminished 7th	64	65	66			Dim 67 / Maj 68		69		70		71
Major 6th	72	73	74		75			76				
Minor 6th	77	78	79		80			81				

SHUFFLE PLAY

Although I recommend a structured approach (as described above) for most players, you can sometimes find yourself in a harmonic rut. If you always order the same food item at a restaurant, every once in a while it's nice to order something completely different from "the usual." Put your CD player on "shuffle play" and prepare for a fun ride through all kinds of different chords. This is the harmonic equivalent of the "Chef's Surprise"!

TWO MORE ANALOGIES

As an educator, one of my favorite teaching tools is the use of analogies to convey ideas. Below are two short analogies regarding harmony.

THE FRENCH FRIED C7 CHORD

While having lunch with a student, we were discussing the concept of synesthesia. At that point, I picked up a french fry from the plate in front of me and told him to pretend that it was a C dominant seventh chord. Next, I took the french fry and dipped it into some ketchup. Now it's a C7b9! Next, I dipped it into some guacamole. Now it's a C7b9#11! The ketchup is the flat ninth and the guacamole is the sharp eleventh. We all know the flavor and texture of a french fry. Even if we put ketchup on the french fry, we can tell by the taste that it's a still a french fry, but now there's an additional flavor present as well.

THE HARMONIC GROCERY STORE

Tasting Harmony is like a grocery store of harmony for your ears. The shelves are bursting with all types of harmonic flavors. Just as you wouldn't buy every single item on the shelves on one trip to the store, you wouldn't attempt to sample every single sound on the play-along CD in one sitting.

You simply take as much or as little harmonic content as you need from the CD, whether it's one forty-five second track, or an entire family of chords. When you feel you've digested those sounds and are ready for more, you go back to the CD, just as you'd return to the store and perhaps try a different brand of cornflakes, or maybe even switch to shredded wheat on the next trip!

MORE RESOURCES AVAILABLE ONLINE

If you'd like to read more about my concepts on jazz improvisation, please go to my educational website: www.gregfishmanjazzstudios.com. There are downloadable articles on theory and ear training, as well as a variety of licks and useful practice tips.

CLINICS, SEMINARS AND MASTERCLASSES

For information on my clinics, seminars and masterclasses in the U.S. and internationally, please contact me at:

Greg Fishman Jazz Studios
824 Custer Avenue
Evanston, Illinois 60202
847-334-3634
E-mail: greg@gregfishmanjazzstudios.com | Web: www.gregfishmanjazzstudios.com

Practice Options & Suggestions

PRACTICE OPTION 1 - NOTE MATCHING

TASTING SEVENTHS ON MINOR 7TH CHORDS

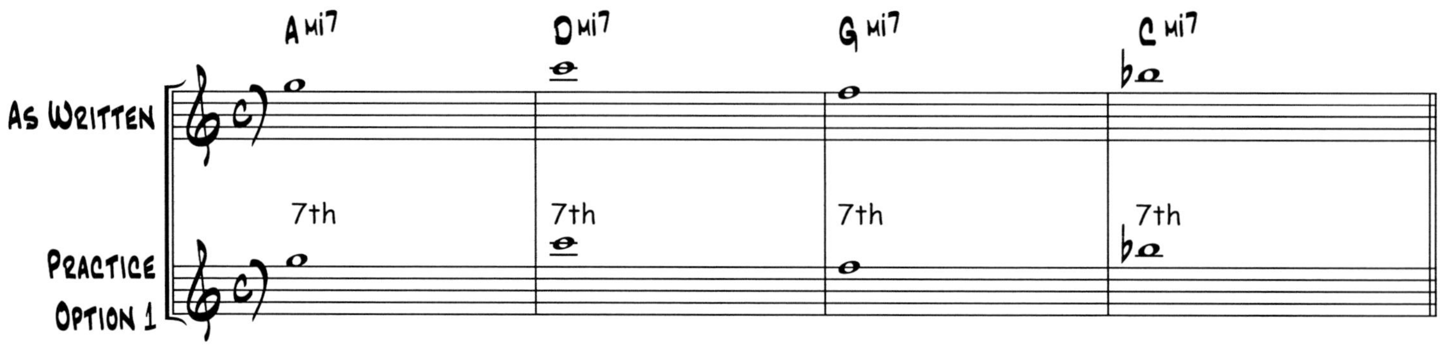

Track 46, p. 41

Practice option one demonstrates the fundamental concept of this book: hearing an individual note in a wide variety of harmonic contexts. Sing (or play) the notes being sung on the play-along CD track and listen to the way they blend in with the sound of the chords being played by the piano. Although each of the eighty-one play-along tracks features whole notes starting on a concert Bb and going through the circle of fourths, the chords which accompany the notes are different for each track. Think of these tracks as representing eighty-one different harmonic flavors.

PRACTICE OPTION 2 - ROOTS

TASTING SEVENTHS ON MINOR 7TH CHORDS

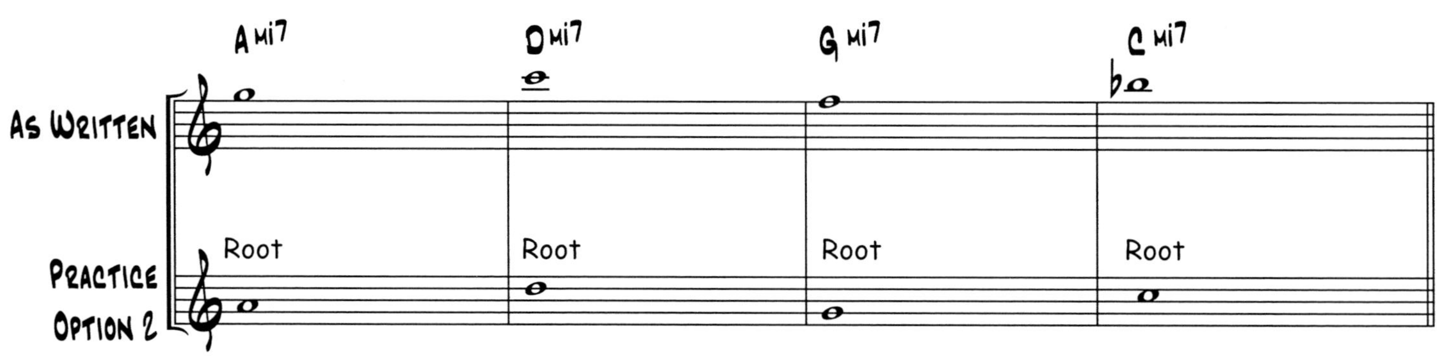

Track 46, p. 41

Sing (or play) the root of the chord while Petra sings other chord tones. This is one of the most important things you can do to strengthen your ear. Hearing the bass note is an essential skill because it provides a musical point of reference that lets your ear measure the harmonic distance to any chord tone. Although the melody for each of the eighty-one tracks starts on a concert Bb, the bass notes are always changing for each track. After listening to a track and focusing on the melody note, repeat the track and focus on the bass note. This approach will give you what I call "the bass player's" perspective.

PRACTICE OPTION 3 - CHORD TONES

TASTING SEVENTHS ON MINOR 7TH CHORDS

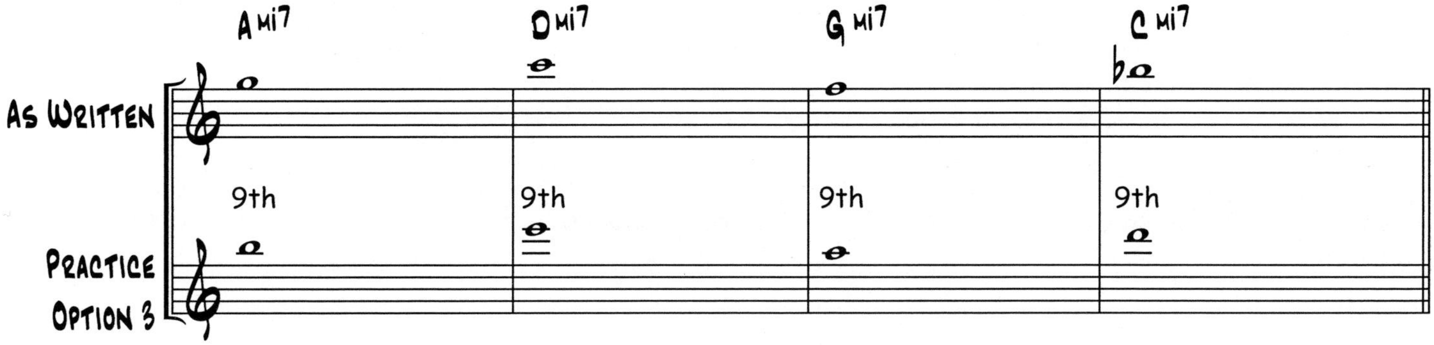

Track 46, p. 41

Sing (or play) any chord tone in the circle of fourths against the note being sung on the recording. In the example above, I demonstrate ninths being played along with the recorded sevenths. This is one of my favorite exercieses.

If you're not sure about the spellings of the chords and would still like to sing different chord tones along with the CD track, there's a simple way to figure out your note. Since all twelve notes are sung on every track, you can simply look at the music for a different track and find your starting pitch.

For example, if you want to sing ninths (as above) along with the sevenths, but you don't know how to spell the chord to the ninth, look at the first chord for the track you're working with. In the example above (track 46) the first chord is Ami7.

To locate the ninth of Ami7, look for the title "Tasting Ninths on Minor 7th Chords" and look for the Ami7 chord symbol. (In this case, you'll find the Ami7 in the ninth measure of the music for track 47, on page 42). When you find it, look at the whole note. In this case it will be a "B" natural. This is your starting note for singing ninths along with the sevenths. Play through the cycle from that note (B) and you'll be playing ninths for the entire track. As long as you stay within the same chord family, you can use this system to look up any chord tones, from the root to the thirteenth of all chords.

PRACTICE OPTION 4 - INTERVALS

TASTING THIRDS ON MINOR 7TH CHORDS

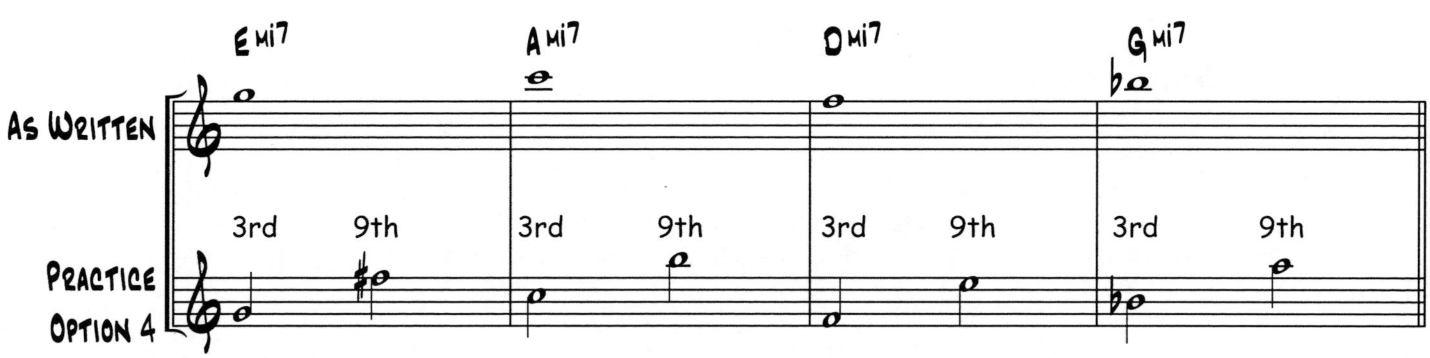

Track 44, p. 40

Option four allows you to practice what I call 'internal intervals" along with each track. For example, if I wanted to practice singing major sevenths in the context of this chord, I could sing a major seventh above the third. Look at the example above and notice the "G" and the "F#" in the first measure (second stave). The "G" up to the "F#" forms the interval of a major seventh. Yet, this is not a major seventh chord; this is a minor seventh chord by name. However, there is a major seventh interval present "internally" when measuring the distance from the third of the chord up to the ninth of the chord. Just as individual notes will have a different sound and flavor when played as different degrees of a chord, (3rd, 5th, 7th, etc.) each interval has a unique flavor when played over a different chord.

In the example below, once again, I've used the major seventh interval internally. This time, I'm using the major seventh interval to bring out the flavor of the thirteenth above the seventh on a dominant chord.

TASTING SEVENTHS ON DOMINANT 7TH CHORDS

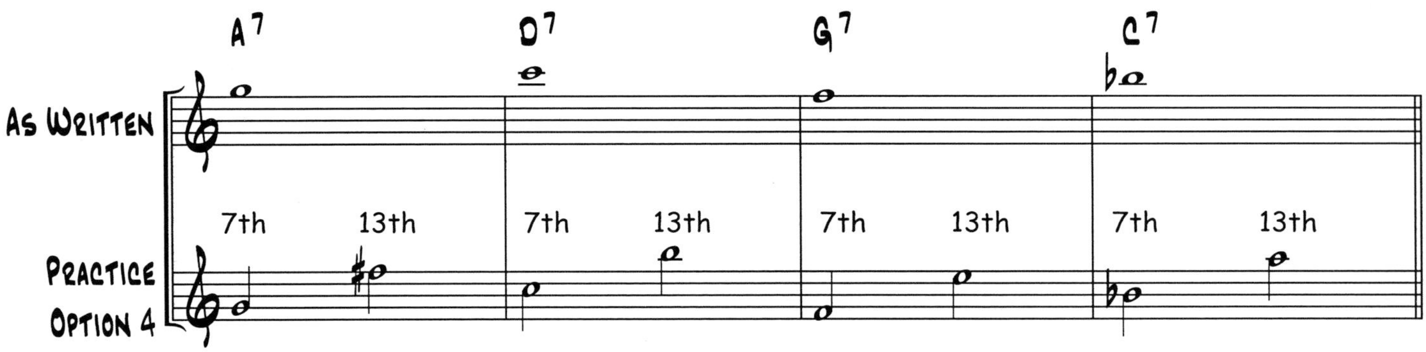

Track 13, p. 24

PRACTICE OPTION 5 - ARPEGGIOS

TASTING ROOTS ON MINOR 7TH CHORDS

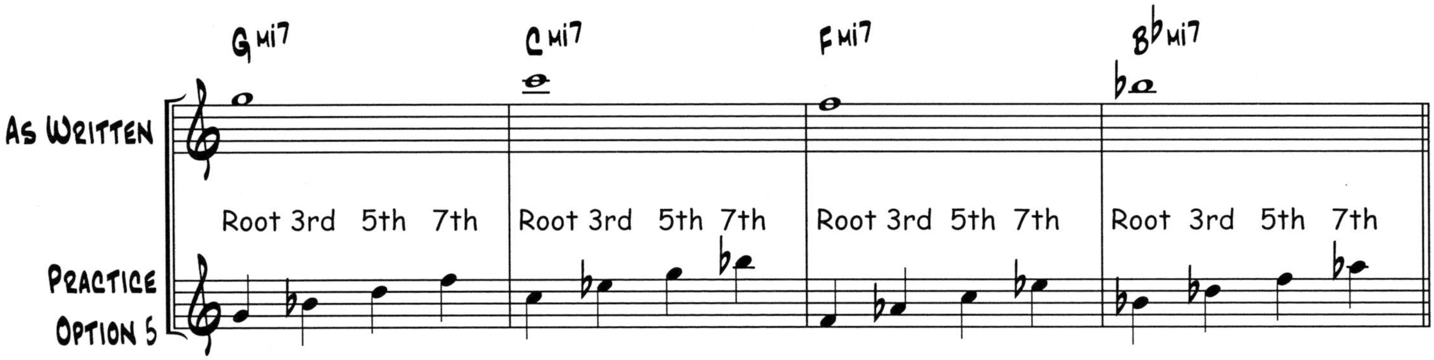

Track 43, p. 40

Practice option five involves arpeggiating the chord against the note being sung on the play-along CD. This is an excellent way to practice hearing the sound of each successive chord tones against a fixed chord tone.

In the example above, the note being held is the root of the chord. If you wanted to practice this same exercise with the third of the chord being held on the CD track, you would select track 44 (tasting thirds on minor 7th chords). See the example on the next page.

TASTING THIRDS ON MINOR 7TH CHORDS

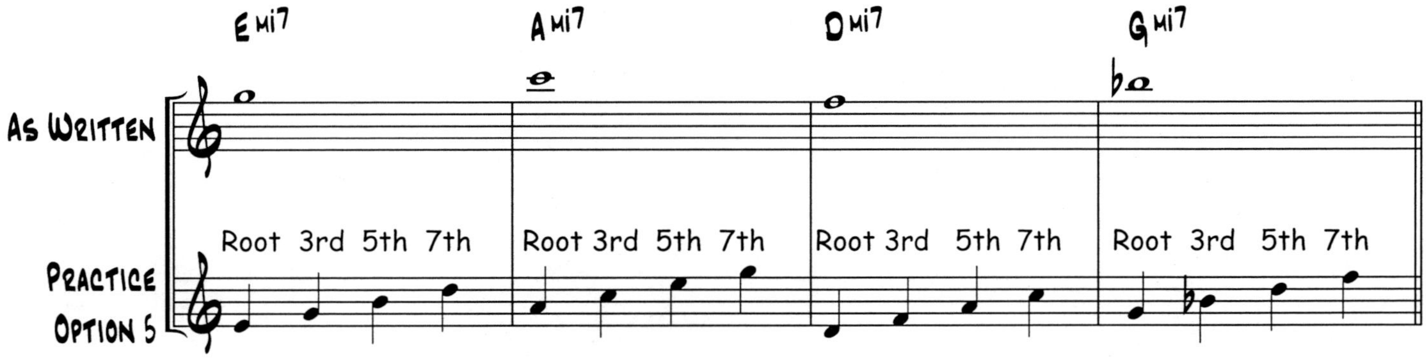

Track 44, p. 40

With practice option five you can also arpeggiate a chord while descending from the melody note, as in the following example:

TASTING SEVENTHS ON MINOR 7TH CHORDS

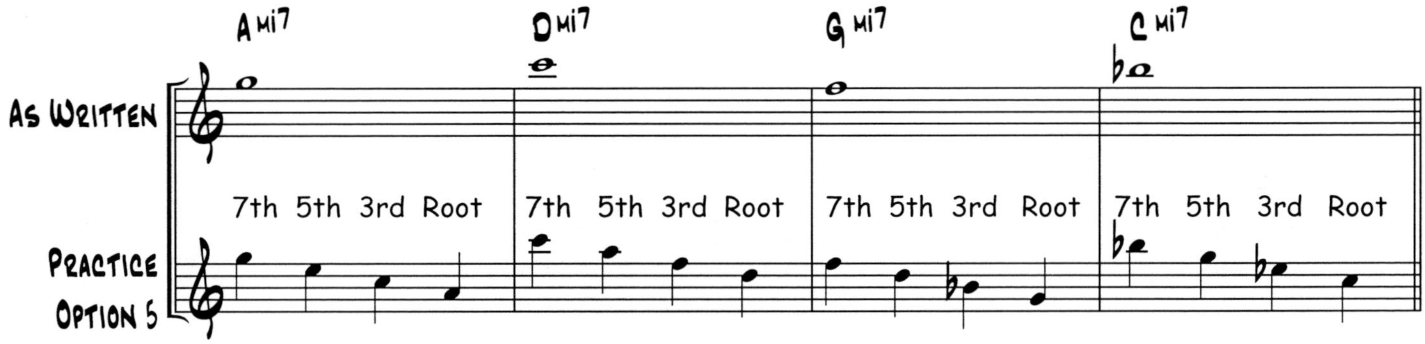

Track 46, p. 41

PRACTICE OPTION 6 - VOICELEADING

TASTING SEVENTHS ON DOMINANT 7TH CHORDS

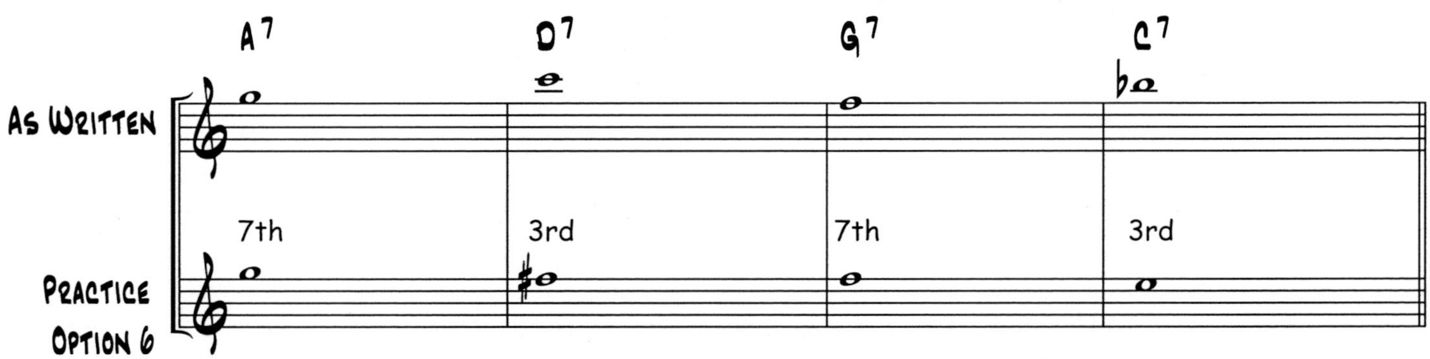

Track 13, p. 24

With practice option six, you can create voiceleading lines. In the example above, you start out on the same pitch as the written example, then lower the note by a half-step in the second measure and then lower the note another half-step in the third measure, once again matching the written note. Continue this pattern to train your ear to hear 7th-to-3rd voiceleading on dominant seventh chords.

TASTING NINTHS ON DOMINANT 7TH CHORDS

Track 14, p. 24

The example above demonstrates an ascending voiceleading line. Continue this pattern over this track to train your ear to hear 9-7-#11 voiceleading in an ascending chromatic line over dominants in the cycle.

PRACTICE OPTION 7 - SCALES

TASTING ROOTS ON MAJOR 7TH CHORDS

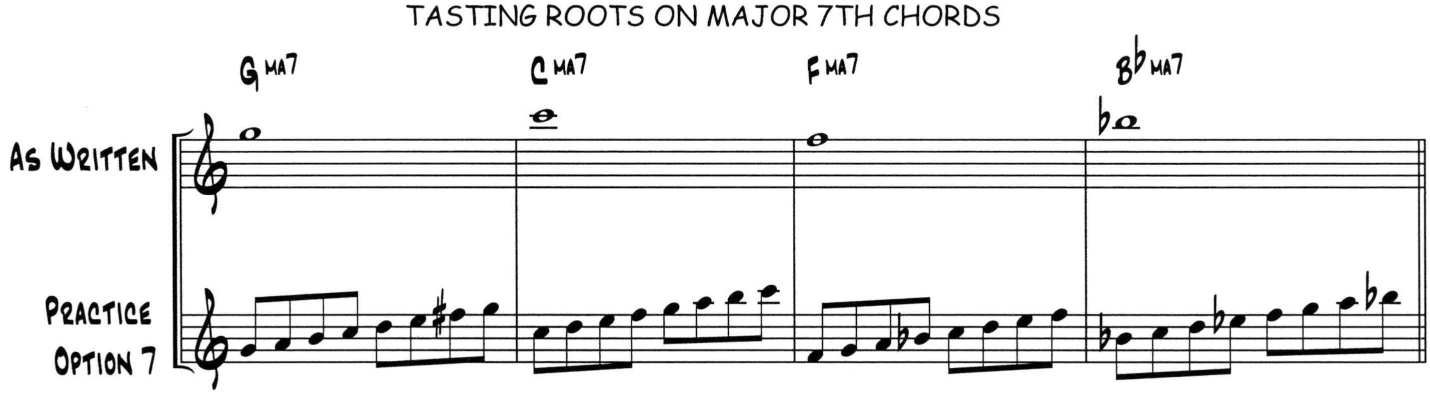

Track 1, p. 18

With practice option seven, you can practice scales while hearing Petra sing one note of the scale. The benefit of this approach is that you can choose whichever chord tone you'd like to hear as a whole note while playing the scale. In the example above, the scale starts on the root of the chord.

TASTING THIRDS ON MINOR 7TH CHORDS

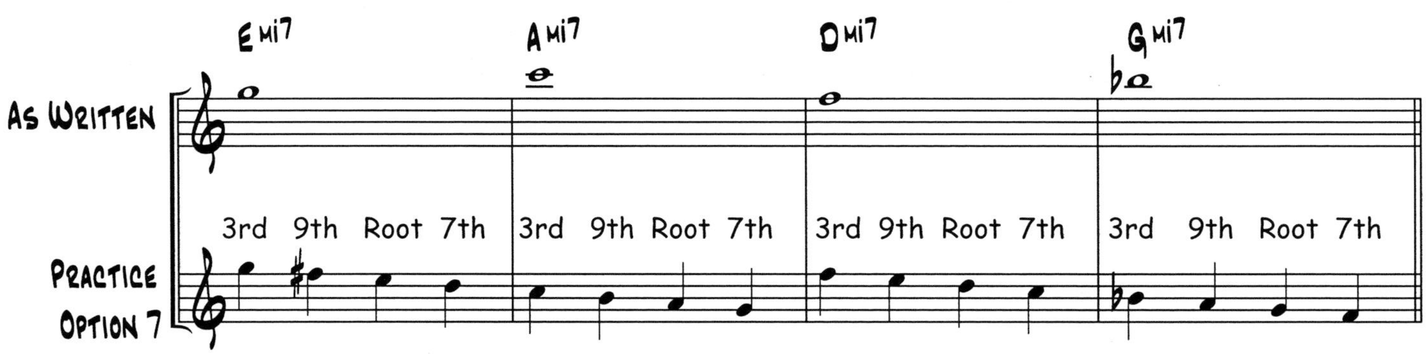

Track 44, p. 40

Practice option seven is also an excellent way to practice specific portions of scales. In the example above, the Dorian scale descends from the third of each chord, descending to the ninth, root and seventh of the chord. If you continue the descending pattern for two measures, as I've done above, you'll create a hybrid scale which sounds like one complete scale played over two measures.

PRACTICE OPTION 8 - LICKS

TASTING ELEVENTHS ON MINOR SEVENTH CHORDS

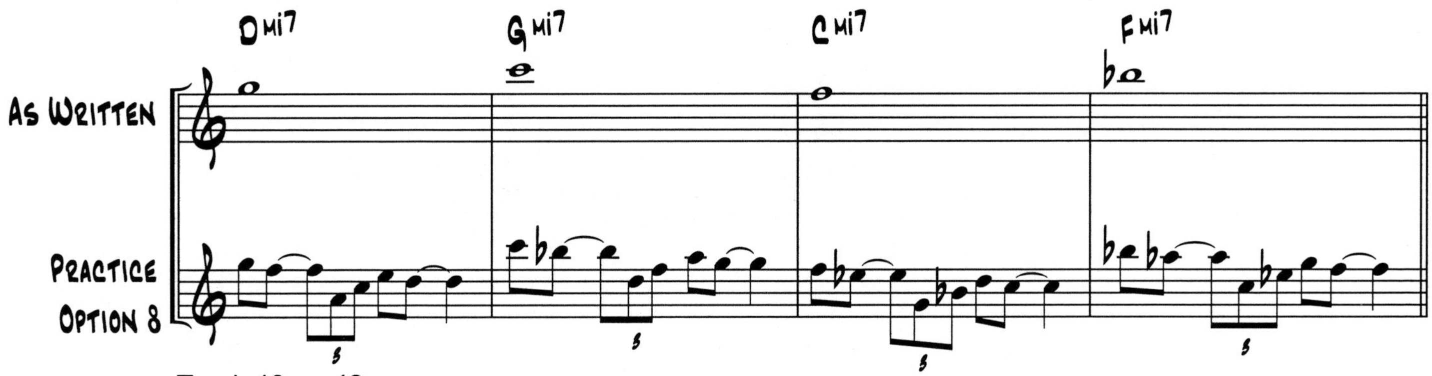

Track 48, p. 42

With option eight, you can practice licks in all twelve keys. Determine the chord tone of the first note of the lick, and then play the lick along with the CD track that matches the same chord tone and chord type.

In the example above, I've used a very common bebop lick and adapted it to the 12/8 time-feel of track forty-eight. This is a minor lick that starts on the eleventh of the chord. Playing the lick along with the track allows your ear to hear the first note of the lick for all four beats of each measure, while hearing the subsequent notes of the lick against the first note. I've found this to be a very fun and useful practice tool.

PRACTICE OPTION 9 - IMPROVISATION

TASTING FIFTHS ON MINOR SEVENTH CHORDS

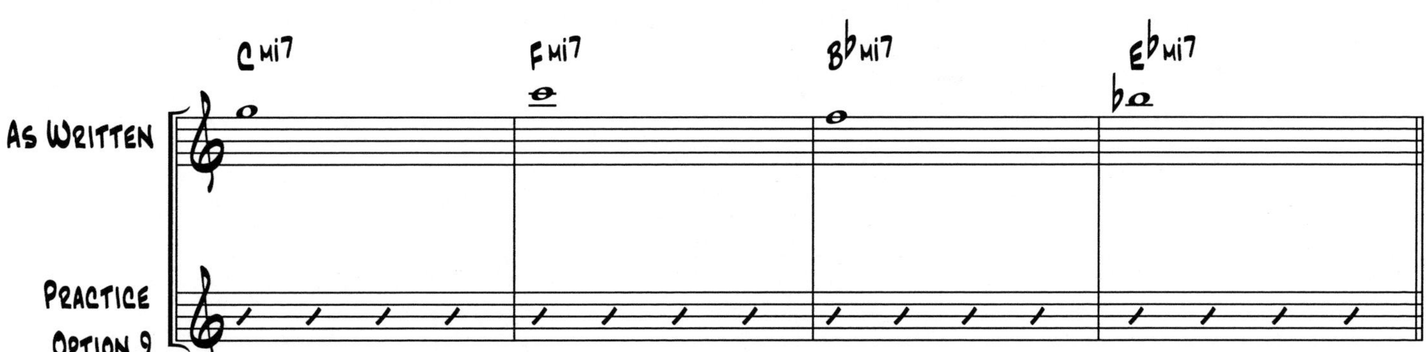

Track 45, p. 41

With the ninth practice option, you can improvise over each track, treating the written note as a "target" note in your improvised lines. You can also mix and match any or all of the nine practice options while singing (or playing) along with each chord. This is a fun and challenging way for advanced players to use *Tasting Harmony.*

DETAILED OVERVIEW OF TASTING HARMONY CD TRACKS

CD Track Number	Chord Family	Degree	Style	Page Number
1	Major 7	Root	Bossa	18
2	Major 7	3rd	Samba	18
3	Major 7	5th	Bossa	19
4	Major 7	7th	Bossa	19
5	Major 7	9th	Bossa	20
6	Major 7	#11th	Latin	20
7	Major 7	13th	Bossa	21
8	Major 7	#5th	Bossa	21
9	Dominant 7	Root	Gospel	22
10	Dominant 7	3rd	Even-Eighths	22
11	Dominant 7	5th	Gospel	23
12	Dominant 7	#5th	Ballad	23
13	Dominant 7	7th	Sneaky Funk	24
14	Dominant 7	9th	12/8 Feel	24
15	Dominant 7	#11th	Ballad	25
16	Dominant 7	13th	Samba	25
17	Dominant 7 Sus	Root	Quasi-Bossa	26
18	Dominant 7 Sus	3rd	Samba	26
19	Dominant 7 Sus	5th	Gospel	27
20	Dominant 7 Sus	7th	Two-Feel	27
21	Dominant 7 Sus	9th	Straight 8th	28
22	Dominant 7 Sus	b9th	Ballad	28
23	Dominant 7 Sus	11th	12/8 Feel	29
24	Dominant 7 Sus	13th	Shuffle	29
25	Dominant 7b9	Root	Bossa	30
26	Dominant 7b9	3rd	Bossa	30
27	Dominant 7b9	5th	Samba	31
28	Dominant 7b9	#5th	Swing	31
29	Dominant 7b9	7th	Even 8th	32
30	Dominant 7b9	b9th	Bossa	32
31	Dominant 7b9	#9th	Bossa	33
32	Dominant 7b9	#11th	12/8 Feel	33
33	Dominant 7b9	13th	Even 8th	34
34	Dominant 7#9	Root	Rock	35
35	Dominant 7#9	3rd	Bossa	35
36	Dominant 7#9	5th	Funk	35
37	Dominant 7#9	#5th	Samba	36
38	Dominant 7#9	7th	Funky Bossa	37
39	Dominant 7#9	b9th	Swing	37
40	Dominant 7#9	#9th	Samba	38

41	Dominant 7#9	#11th	Even 8th	38
42	Dominant 7#9	13th	Funk	39
43	Minor 7	Root	Swing	40
44	Minor 7	3rd	Straight 8th	40
45	Minor 7	5th	Samba	41
46	Minor 7	7th	Swing	41
47	Minor 7	9th	12/8 Feel	42
48	Minor 7	11th	12/8 Feel	42
49	Minor 7	13th	Bossa	43
50	Minor w/Maj 7	Root	Bossa	44
51	Minor w/Maj 7	3rd	Swing	44
52	Minor w/Maj 7	5th	Swing	45
53	Minor w/Maj 7	7th	Bossa	45
54	Minor w/Maj 7	9th	12/8 Feel	46
55	Minor w/Maj 7	11th	Swing	46
56	Minor w/Maj 7	13th	Samba	47
57	Minor 7b5	Root	Swing	48
58	Minor 7b5	3rd	Bossa	48
59	Minor 7b5	5th	Samba	49
60	Minor 7b5	7th	Broken Swing	49
61	Minor 7b5	9th	Bossa	50
62	Minor 7b5	11th	Samba	50
63	Minor 7b5	13th	Broken Swing	51
64	Diminished 7	Root	Bossa	52
65	Diminished 7	3rd	Funk	52
66	Diminished 7	5th	Bossa	53
67	Diminished 7	7th	Swing	53
68	Diminished 7	Major 7th	Even 8th	54
69	Diminished 7	9th	Rock	54
70	Diminished 7	11th	Bossa	55
71	Diminished 7	13th	Bossa	55
72	Major 6	Root	Swing	56
73	Major 6	3rd	Bossa	56
74	Major 6	5th	Samba	57
75	Major 6	6th	Bossa	57
76	Major 6	9th	Samba	58
77	Minor 6	Root	Two-Feel	59
78	Minor 6	3rd	Swing	59
79	Minor 6	5th	Bossa	60
80	Minor 6	6th	Bossa	60
81	Minor 6	9th	Swing	61

TASTING ROOTS ON MAJOR 7TH CHORDS

TRACK 1 - BOSSA

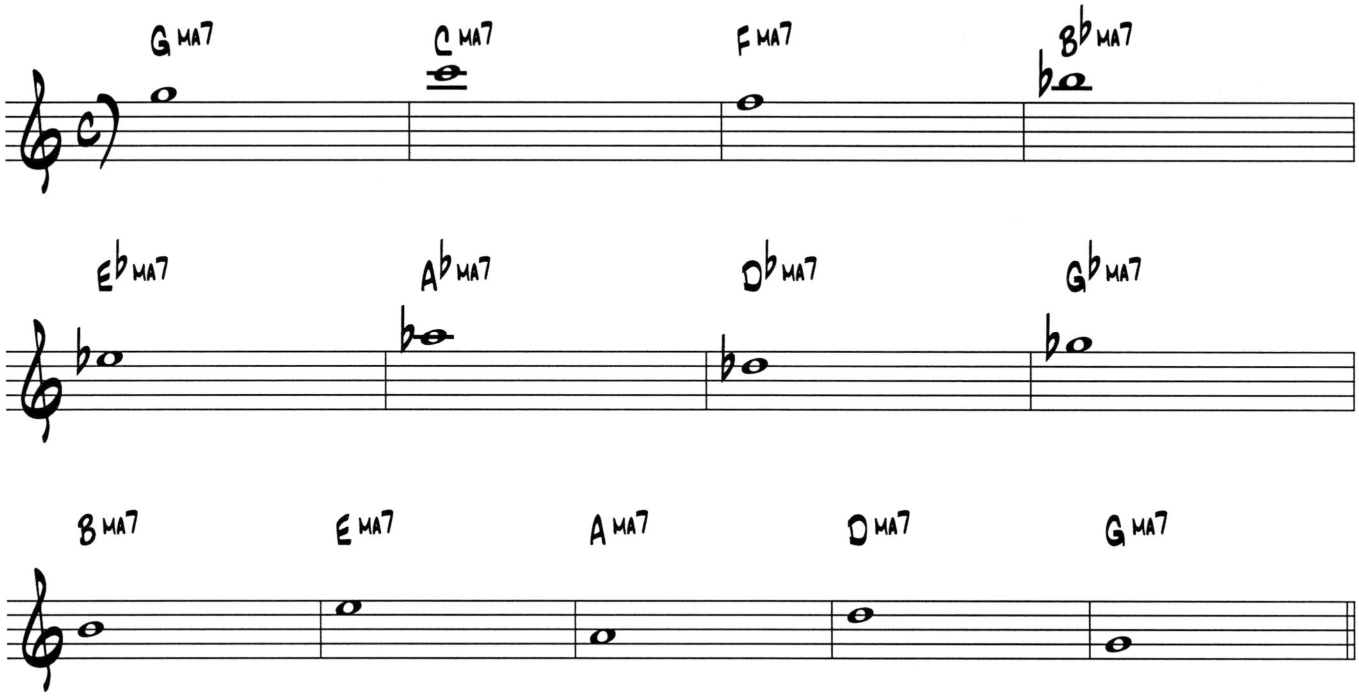

TASTING THIRDS ON MAJOR 7TH CHORDS

TRACK 2 - SAMBA

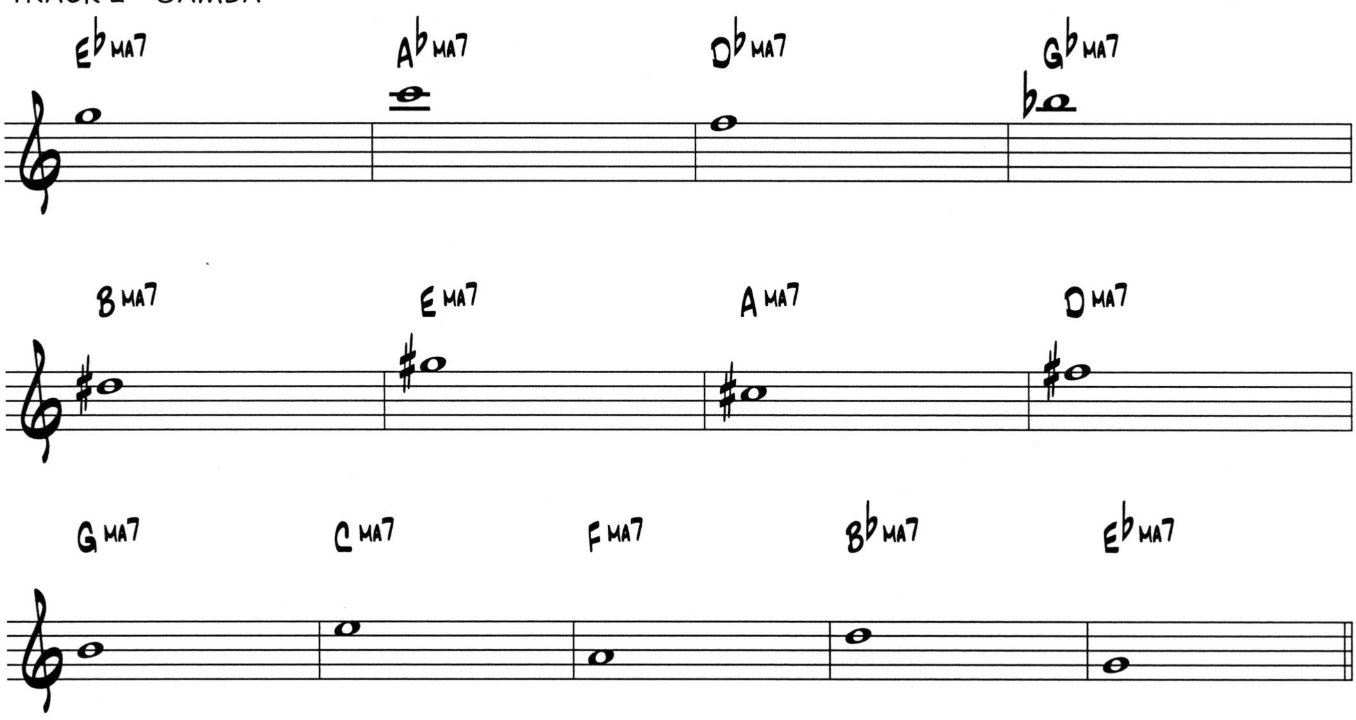

TASTING FIFTHS ON MAJOR 7TH CHORDS

TRACK 3 - BOSSA

TASTING SEVENTHS ON MAJOR 7TH CHORDS

TRACK 4 - BOSSA

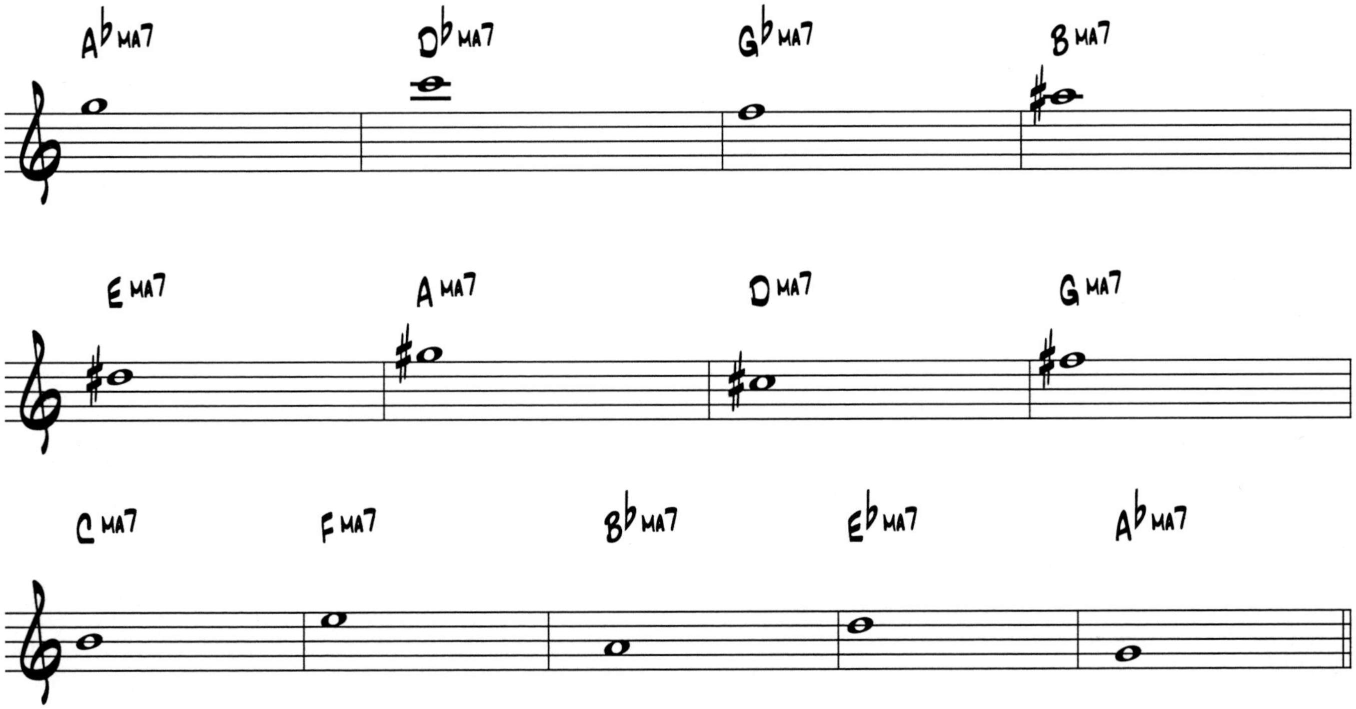

TASTING NINTHS ON MAJOR 7TH CHORDS

TRACK 5 - BOSSA

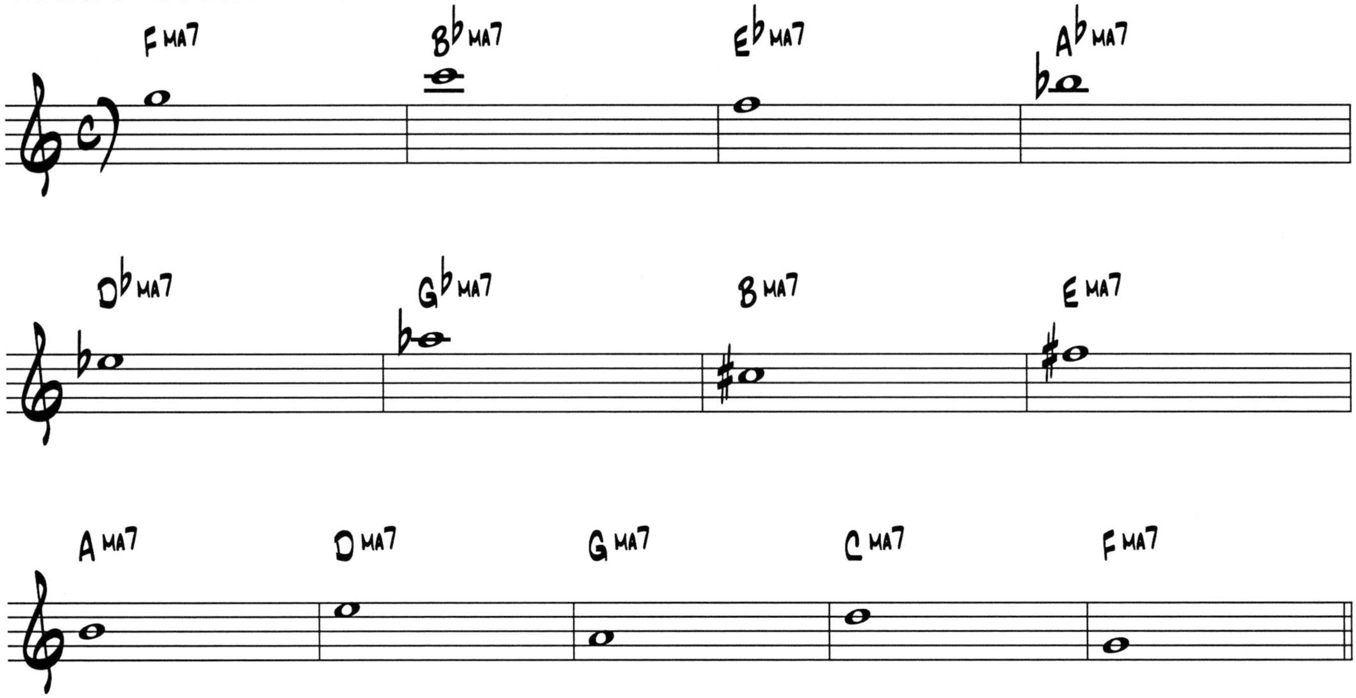

TASTING SHARP ELEVENTHS ON MAJOR 7TH CHORDS

TRACK 6 - LATIN

TASTING THIRTEENTHS ON MAJOR 7TH CHORDS

TRACK 7 - BOSSA

TASTING SHARP FIFTHS ON MAJOR 7TH #5 CHORDS

TRACK 8 - BOSSA

TASTING ROOTS ON DOMINANT 7TH CHORDS

TRACK 9 - GOSPEL

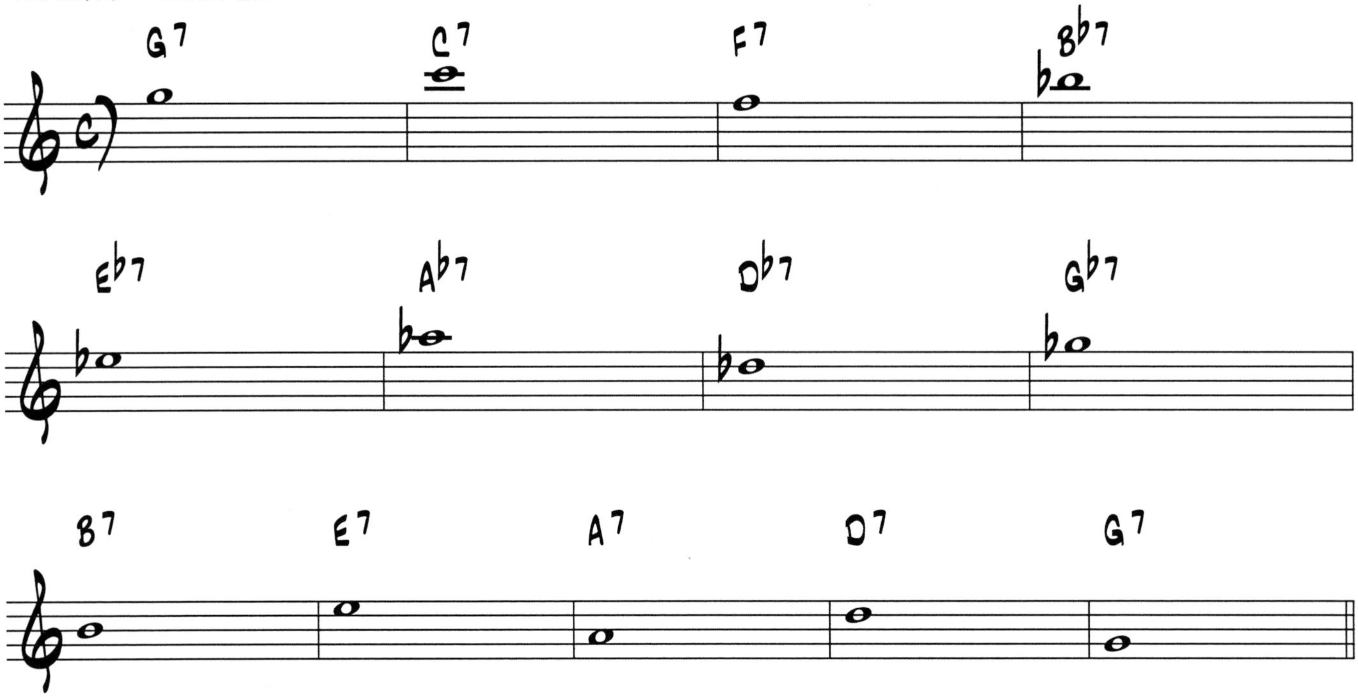

TASTING THIRDS ON DOMINANT 7TH CHORDS

TRACK 10 - EVEN 8THS

TASTING FIFTHS ON DOMINANT 7TH CHORDS

TRACK 11 - GOSPEL

TASTING SHARP FIFTHS ON DOMINANT 7TH CHORDS

TRACK 12 - FLOATING BALLAD

TASTING SEVENTHS ON DOMINANT 7TH CHORDS

TRACK 13 - SNEAKY FUNK

TASTING NINTHS ON DOMINANT 7TH CHORDS

TRACK 14 - 12/8 FEEL

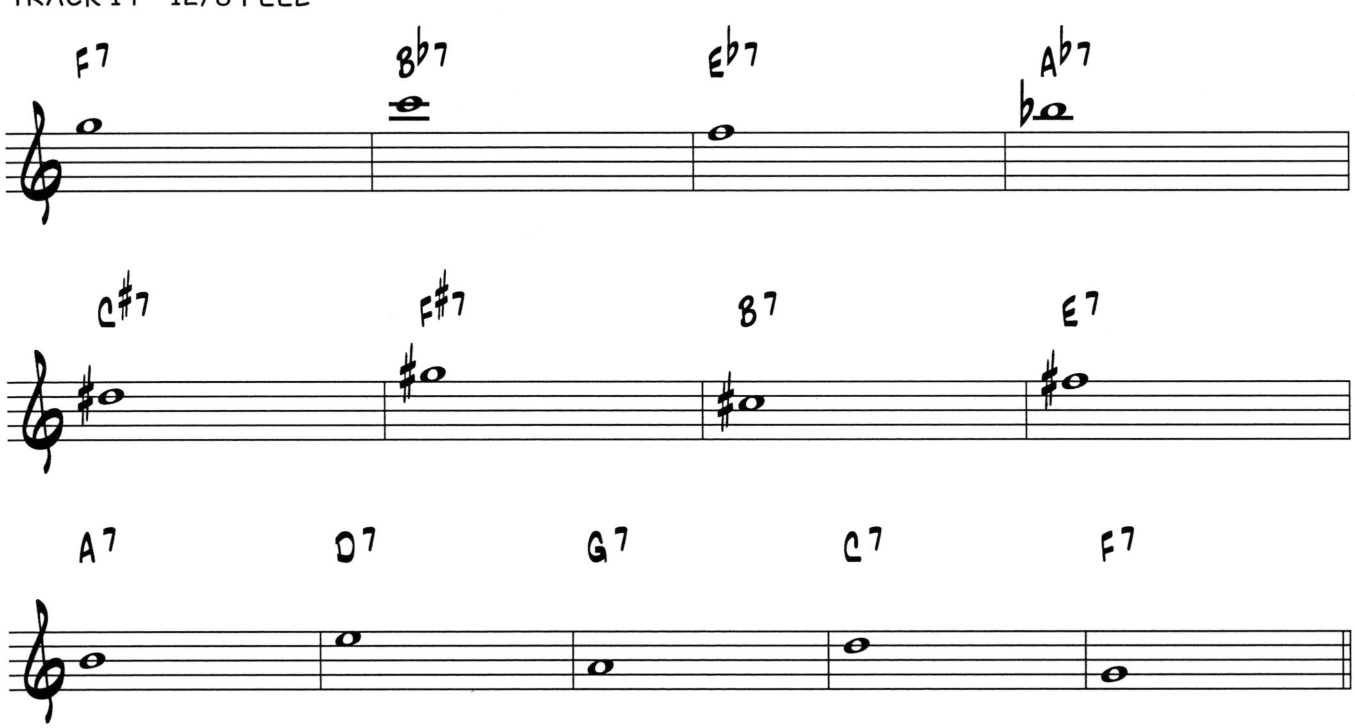

TASTING SHARP ELEVENTHS ON DOMINANT 7TH CHORDS

TRACK 15 - FLOATING BALLAD

TASTING THIRTEENTHS ON DOMINANT 7TH CHORDS

TRACK 16 - SAMBA

TASTING ROOTS ON DOMINANT 7TH SUS CHORDS

TRACK 17 - QUASI-BOSSA

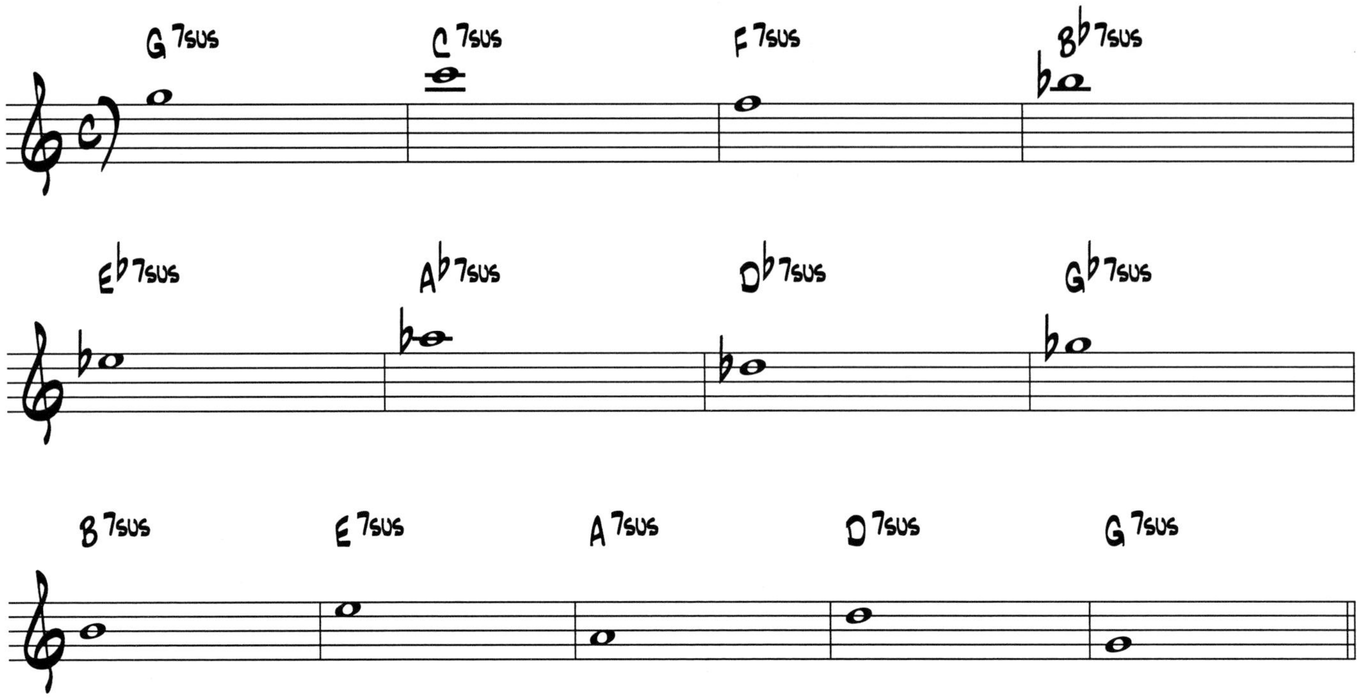

TASTING THIRDS ON DOMINANT 7TH SUS CHORDS

TRACK 18 - SAMBA

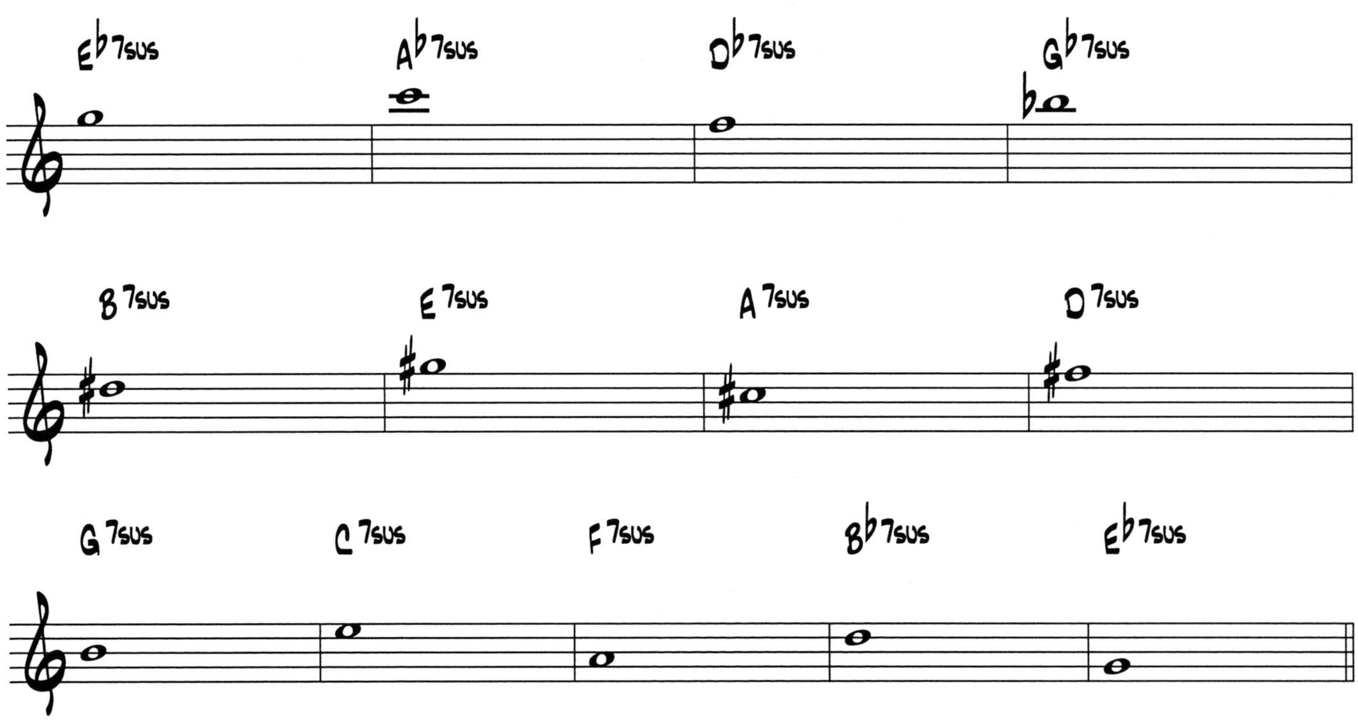

TASTING FIFTHS ON DOMINANT 7TH SUS CHORDS

TRACK 19 - GOSPEL

TASTING SEVENTHS ON DOMINANT 7TH SUS CHORDS

TRACK 20 -TWO FEEL

TASTING NINTHS ON DOMINANT 7TH SUS CHORDS

TRACK 21 - STRAIGHT 8TH

TASTING FLAT NINTHS ON DOMINANT 7TH SUS CHORDS

TRACK 22 - BALLAD

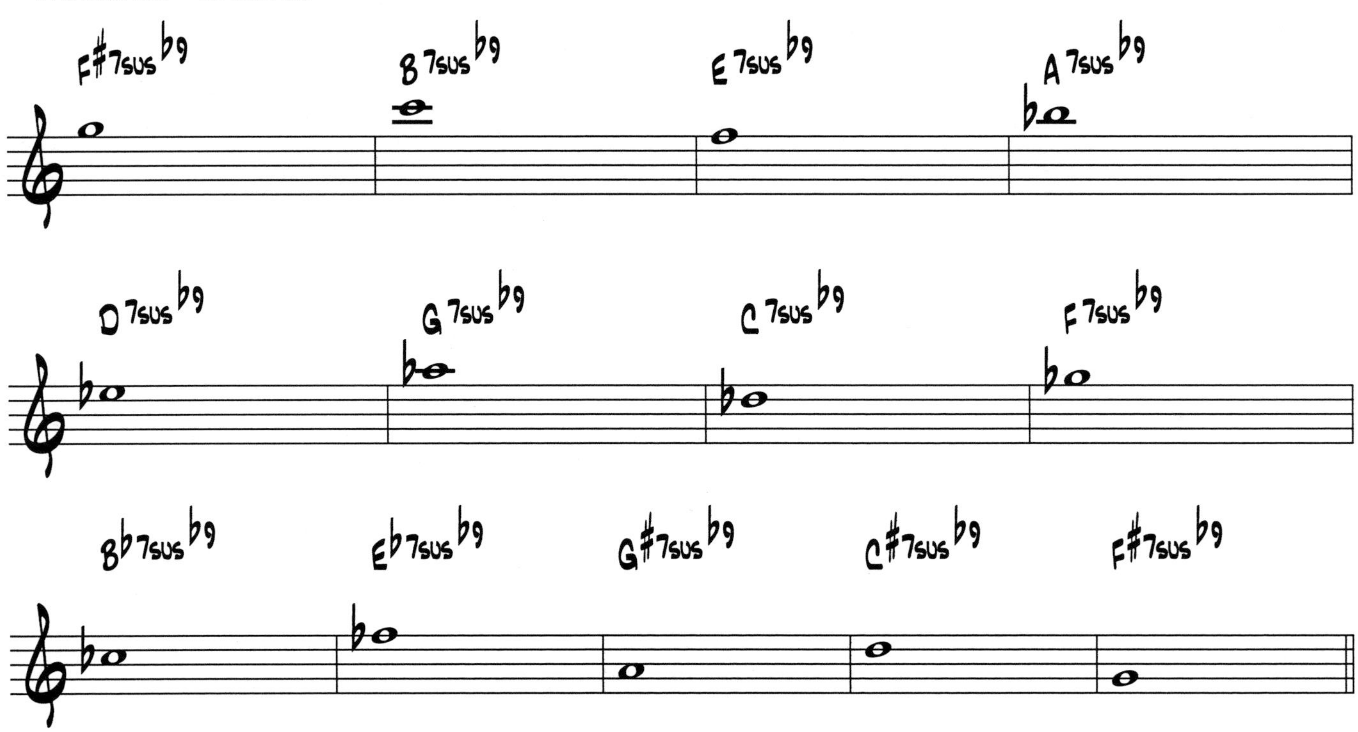

TASTING ELEVENTHS ON DOMINANT 7TH SUS CHORDS

TRACK 23 - 12/8 FEEL

TASTING THIRTEENTHS ON DOMINANT 7TH SUS CHORDS

TRACK 24 -SHUFFLE

TASTING ROOTS ON DOMINANT 7b9 CHORDS

TRACK 25 - BOSSA

TASTING THIRDS ON DOMINANT 7b9 CHORDS

TRACK 26 - BOSSA

TASTING FIFTHS ON DOMINANT 7b9 CHORDS

TRACK 27 - SAMBA

TASTING SHARP FIFTHS ON DOMINANT 7b9 CHORDS

TRACK 28 - SWING

TASTING SEVENTHS ON DOMINANT 7b9 CHORDS

TRACK 29 - EVEN-EIGHTHS

TASTING FLAT NINTHS ON DOMINANT 7b9 CHORDS

TRACK 30 - BOSSA

TASTING SHARP NINTHS ON DOMINANT 7b9 CHORDS

TRACK 31 - BOSSA

TASTING SHARP ELEVENTHS ON DOMINANT 7b9 CHORDS

TRACK 32 - 12/8 FEEL

TASTING THIRTEENTHS ON DOMINANT 7b9 CHORDS

TRACK 33 - EVEN 8THS

TASTING ROOTS ON DOMINANT 7#9 CHORDS

TRACK 34 - ROCK

TASTING THIRDS ON DOMINANT 7#9 CHORDS

TRACK 35 - BOSSA

TASTING FIFTHS ON DOMINANT 7#9 CHORDS

TRACK 36 - FUNK

TASTING SHARP FIFTHS ON DOMINANT 7b#9 CHORDS

TRACK 37 - SAMBA

TASTING SEVENTHS ON DOMINANT 7#9 CHORDS

TRACK 38 - FUNKY BOSSA

TASTING FLAT NINTHS ON DOMINANT 7#9 CHORDS

TRACK 39 - SWING

TASTING SHARP NINTHS ON DOMINANT 7#9 CHORDS

TRACK 40 - SAMBA

TASTING SHARP ELEVENTHS ON DOMINANT 7#9 CHORDS

TRACK 41 - EVEN EIGHTHS

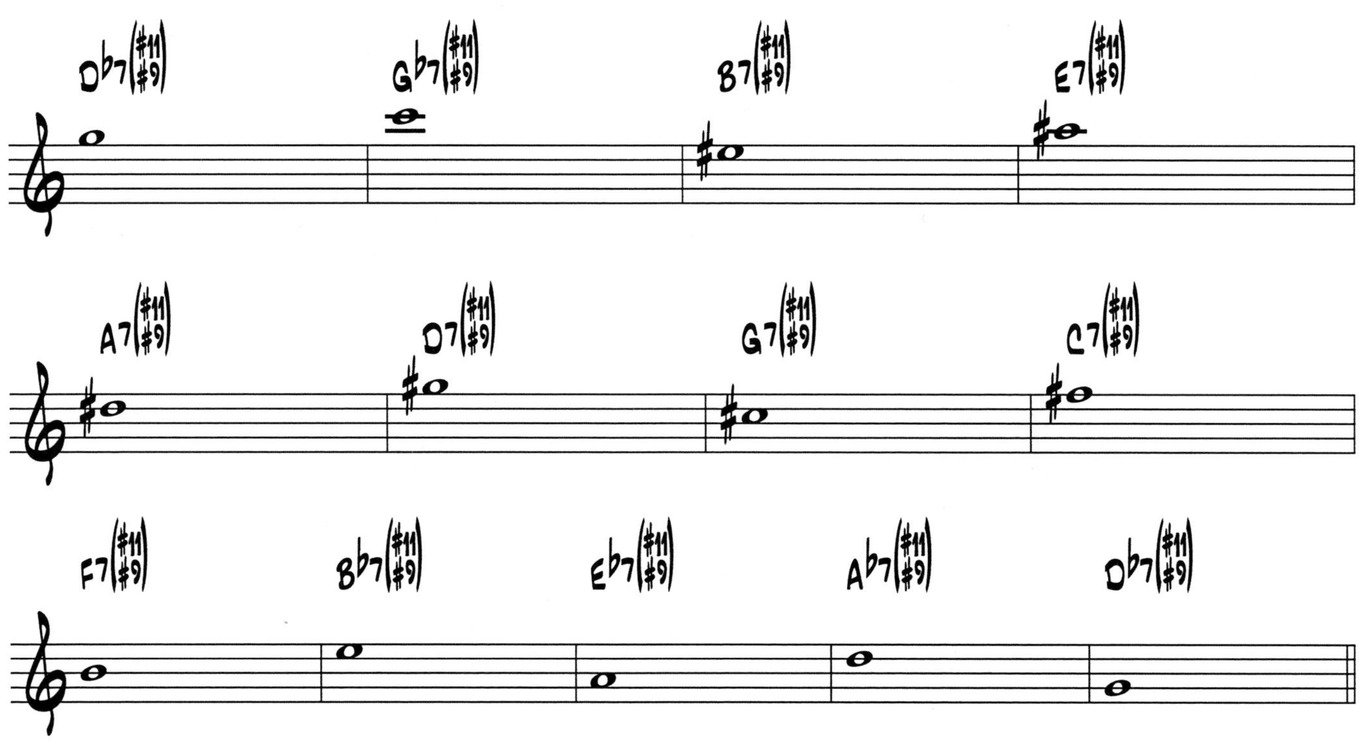

TASTING THIRTEENTHS ON DOMINANT 7#9 CHORDS

TRACK 42 - FUNK

TASTING ROOTS ON MINOR 7TH CHORDS

TRACK 43 - SWING

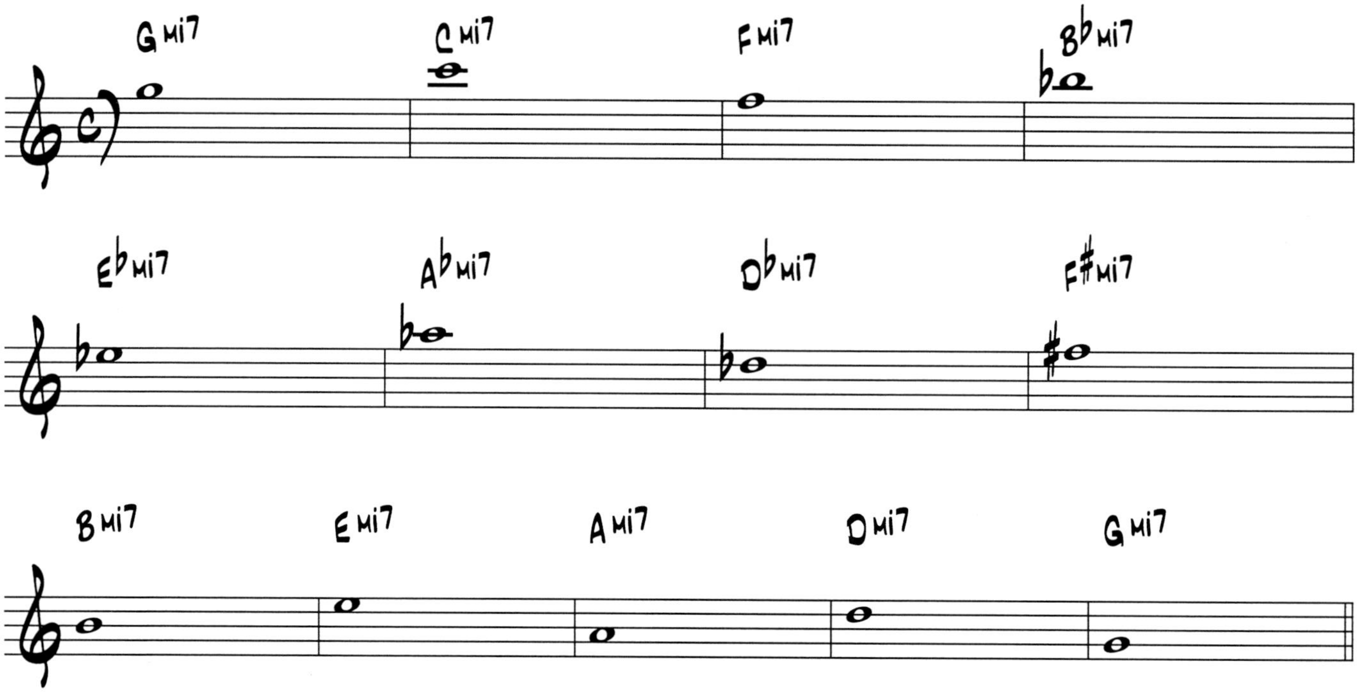

TASTING THIRDS ON MINOR 7TH CHORDS

TRACK 44 - STRAIGHT-EIGHTH

TASTING FIFTHS ON MINOR 7TH CHORDS

TRACK 45 - SAMBA

TASTING SEVENTHS ON MINOR 7TH CHORDS

TRACK 46 -SWING

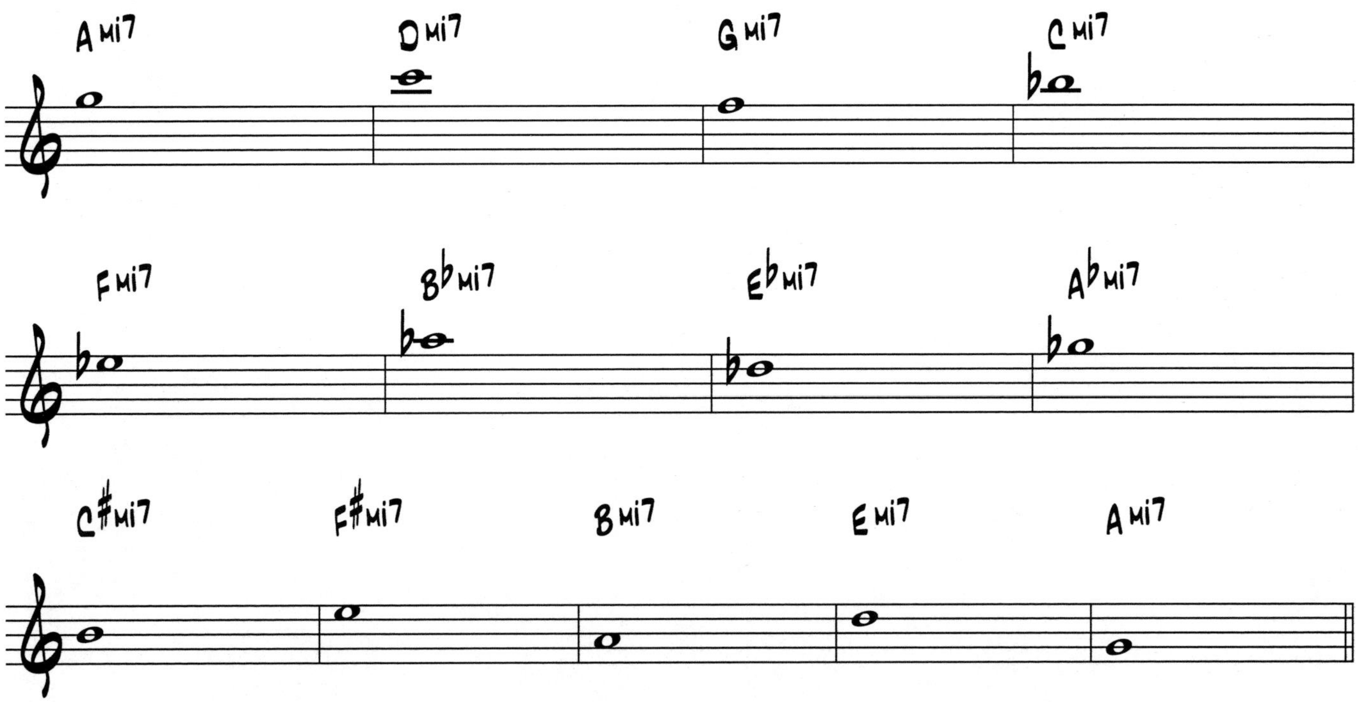

TASTING NINTHS ON MINOR 7TH CHORDS

TRACK 47 - 12/8 FEEL

TASTING ELEVENTHS ON MINOR 7TH CHORDS

TRACK 48 - 12/8 FEEL

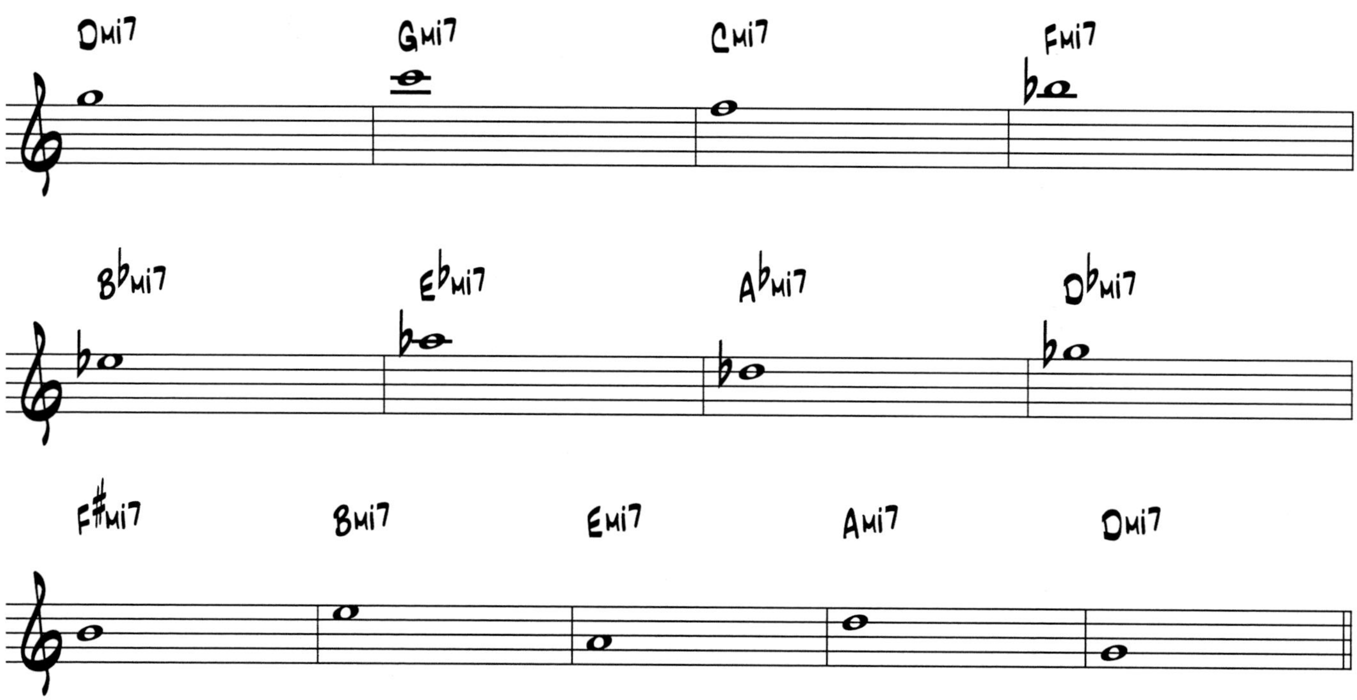

TASTING THIRTEENTHS ON MINOR 7TH CHORDS

TRACK 49 - BOSSA

TASTING ROOTS ON MINOR w/Maj7 CHORDS

TRACK 50 - BOSSA

TASTING THIRDS ON MINOR w/Maj7 CHORDS

TRACK 51 - SWING

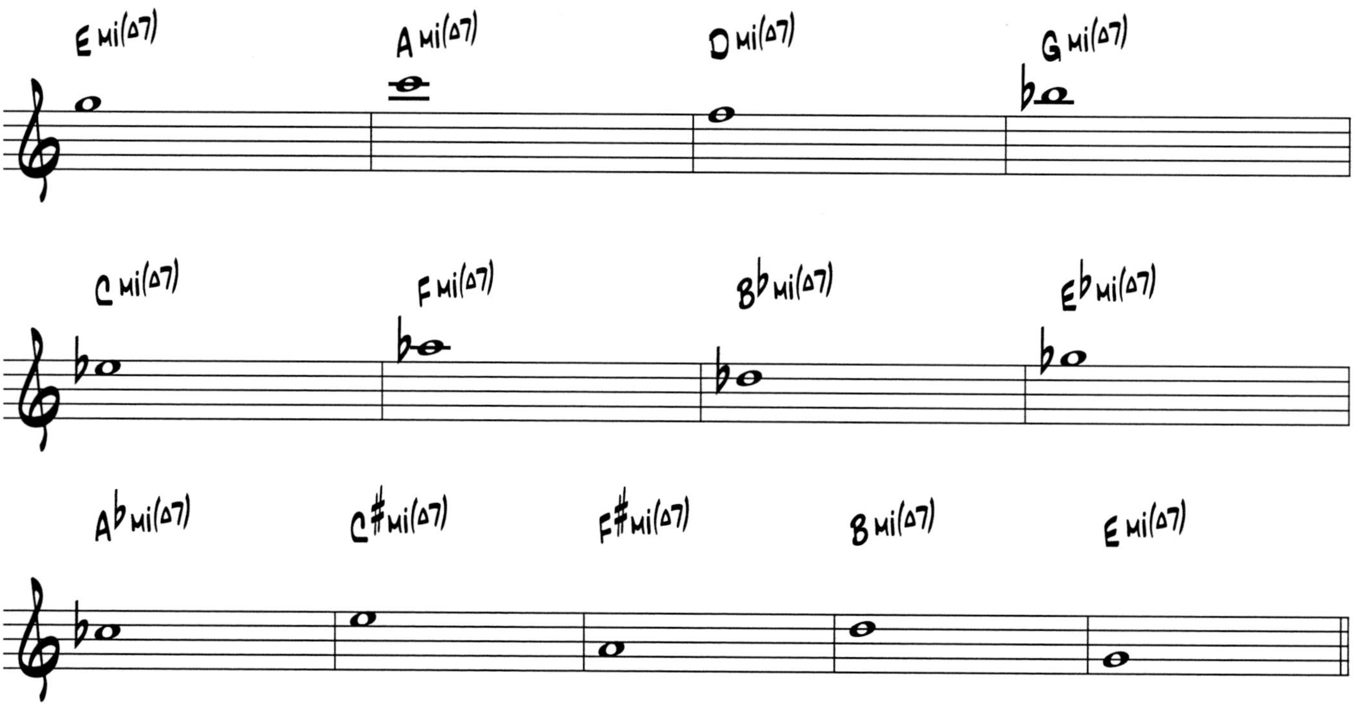

TASTING FIFTHS ON MINOR w/Maj7 CHORDS

TRACK 52 - SWING

TASTING SEVENTHS ON MINOR w/Maj7 CHORDS

TRACK 53 - BOSSA

TASTING NINTHS ON MINOR w/Maj7 CHORDS

TRACK 54 - 12/8 FEEL

TASTING ELEVENTHS ON MINOR w/Maj7 CHORDS

TRACK 55 - SWING

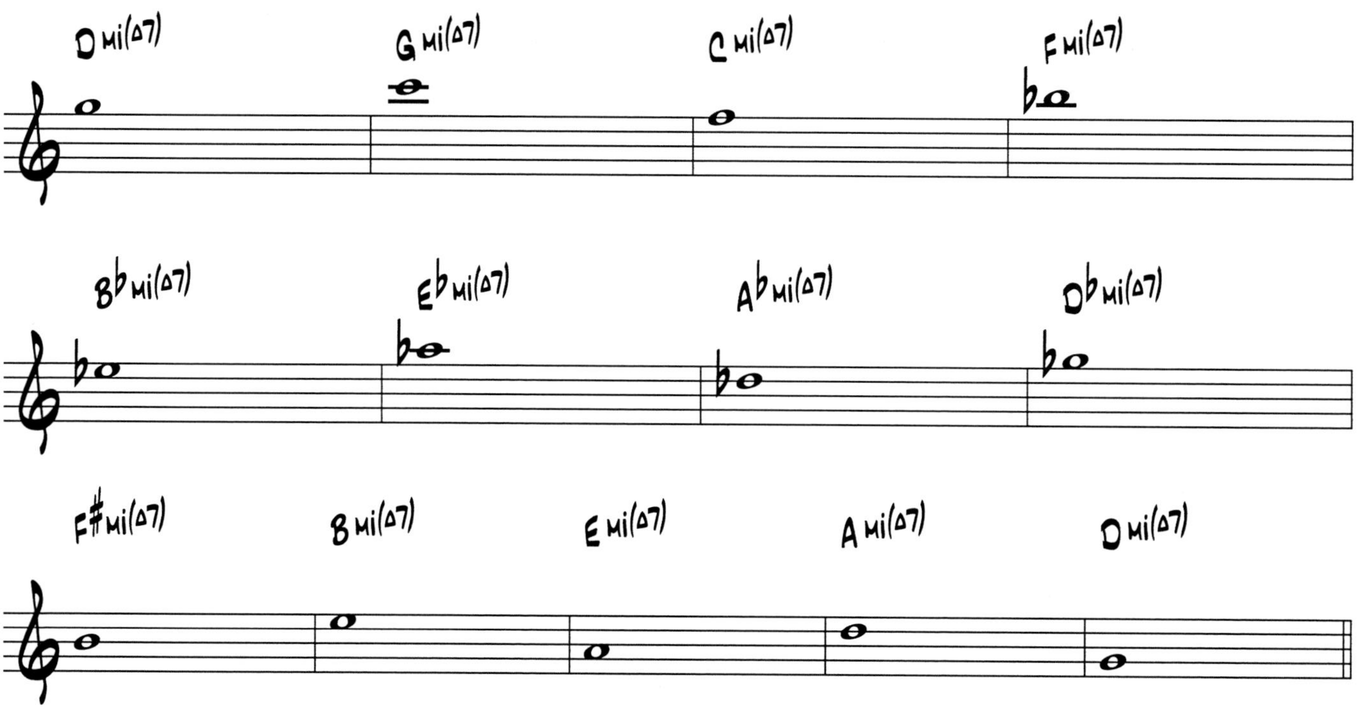

TASTING THIRTEENTHS ON MINOR w/Maj7 CHORDS

TRACK 56 - SAMBA

TASTING ROOTS ON MINOR 7b5 CHORDS

TRACK 57 - SWING

TASTING THIRDS ON MINOR 7b5 CHORDS

TRACK 58 -BOSSA

TASTING FIFTHS ON MINOR 7b5 CHORDS

TRACK 59 - SAMBA

TASTING SEVENTHS ON MINOR 7b5 CHORDS

TRACK 60 - BROKEN SWING

TASTING NINTHS ON MINOR 7b5 CHORDS

TRACK 61 - BOSSA

TASTING ELEVENTHS ON MINOR 7b5 CHORDS

TRACK 62 - SAMBA

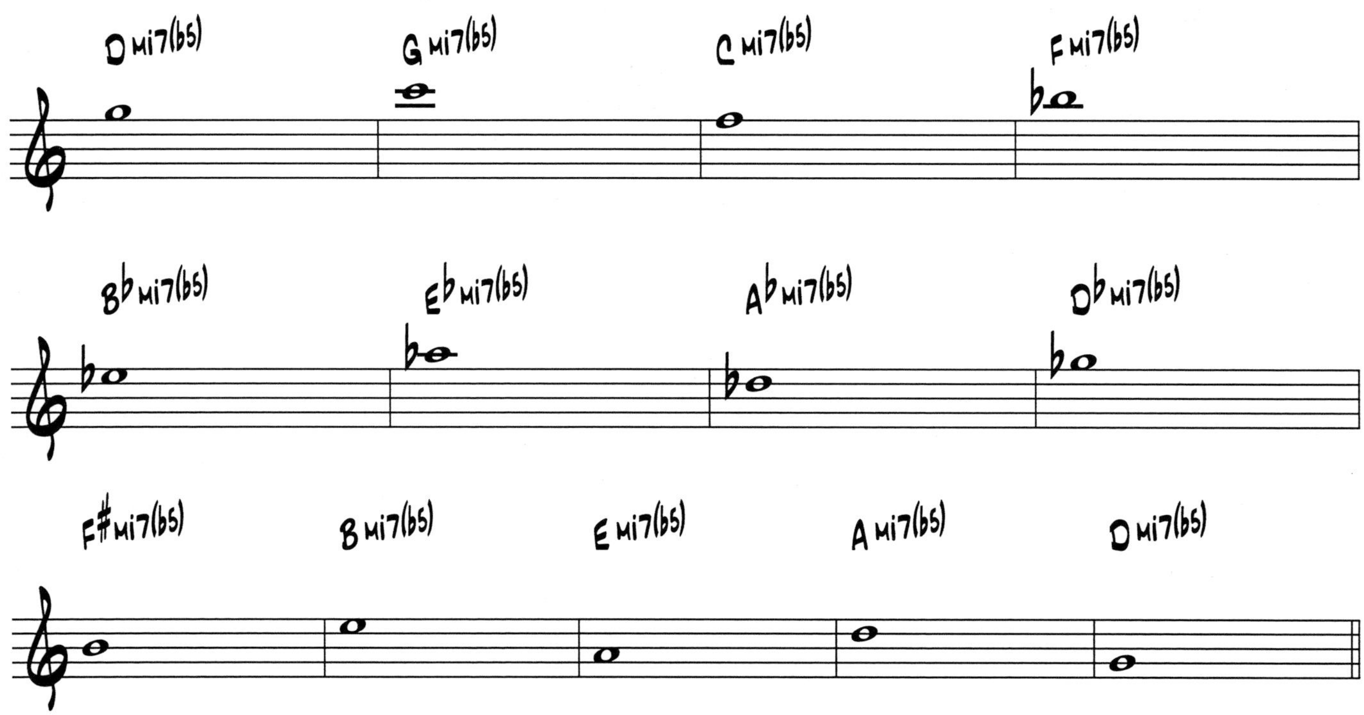

TASTING THIRTEENTHS ON MINOR 7b5 CHORDS

TRACK 63 - BROKEN SWING

TASTING ROOTS ON DIMINISHED 7TH CHORDS

TRACK 64 - BOSSA

TASTING THIRDS ON DIMINISHED 7TH CHORDS

TRACK 65 - FUNK

TASTING FIFTHS ON DIMINISHED 7TH CHORDS

TRACK 66 -BOSSA

TASTING SEVENTHS ON DIMINISHED 7TH CHORDS

TRACK 67 - SWING

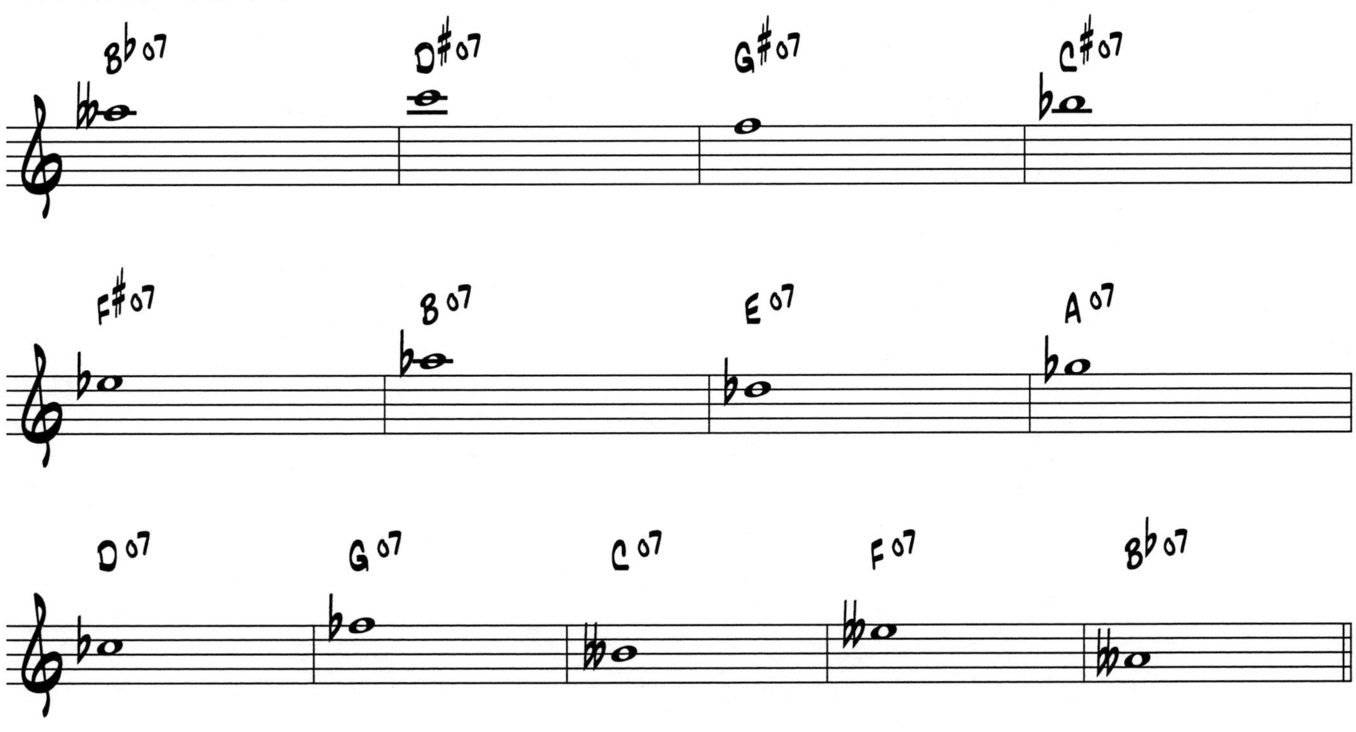

TASTING MAJOR SEVENTHS ON DIMINISHED 7TH CHORDS

TRACK 68 - EVEN-EIGHTHS

TASTING NINTHS ON DIMINISHED 7TH CHORDS

TRACK 69 - ROCK

TASTING ELEVENTHS ON DIMINISHED 7TH CHORDS

TRACK 70 - BOSSA

TASTING THIRTEENTHS ON DIMINISHED 7TH CHORDS

TRACK 71 - BOSSA

TASTING ROOTS ON MAJOR 6TH CHORDS

TRACK 72 -SWING

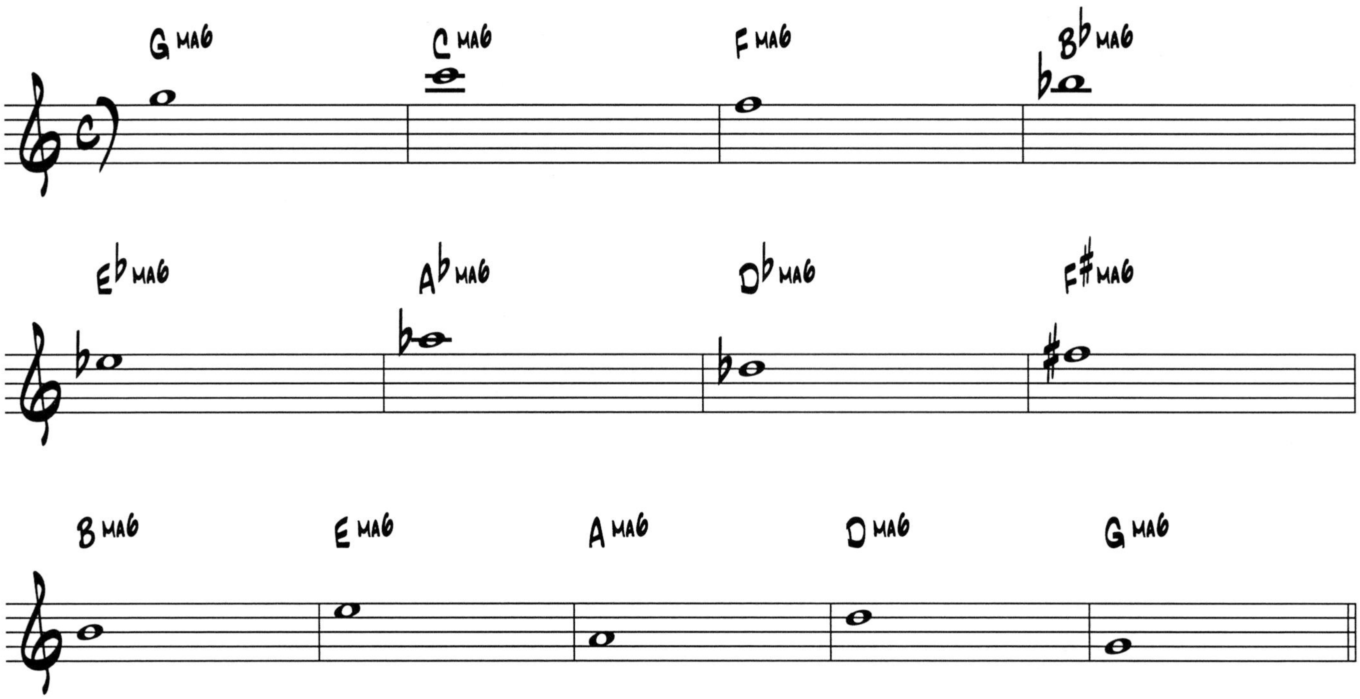

TASTING THIRDS ON MAJOR 6TH CHORDS

TRACK 73 - BOSSA

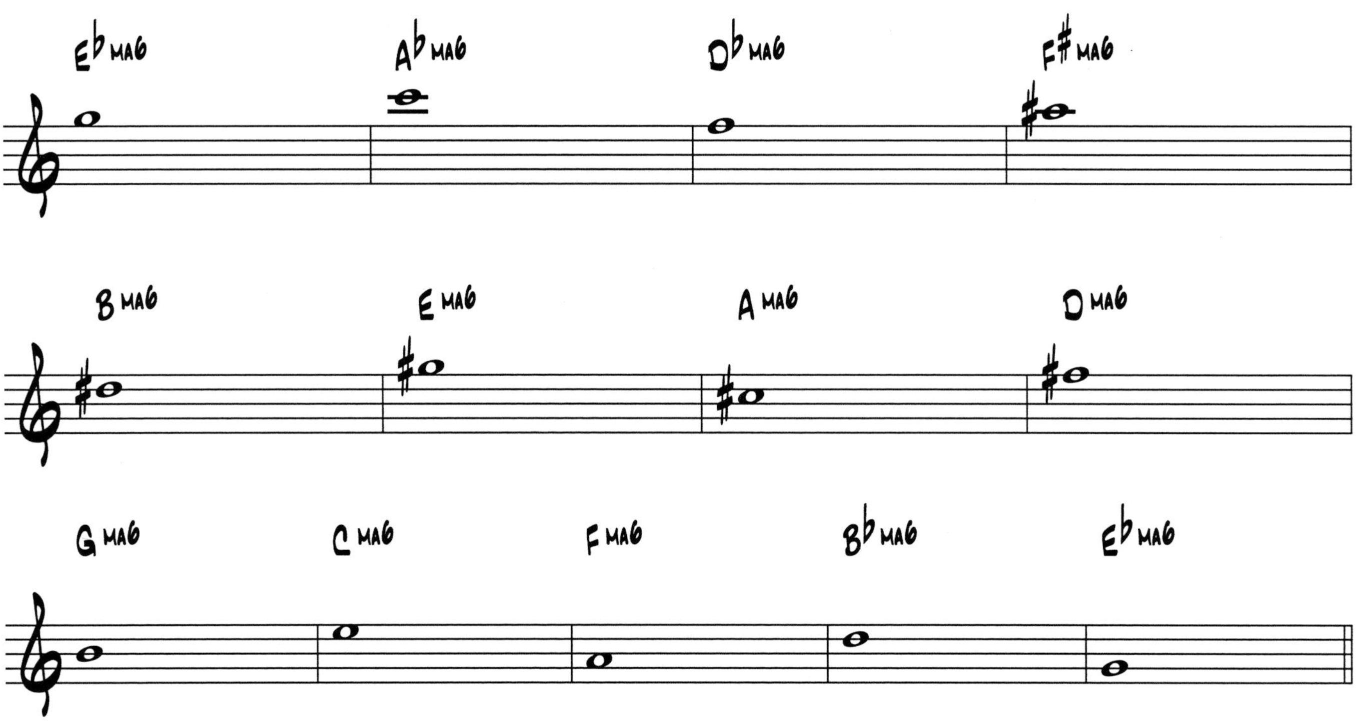

TASTING FIFTHS ON MAJOR 6TH CHORDS

TRACK 74 - SAMBA

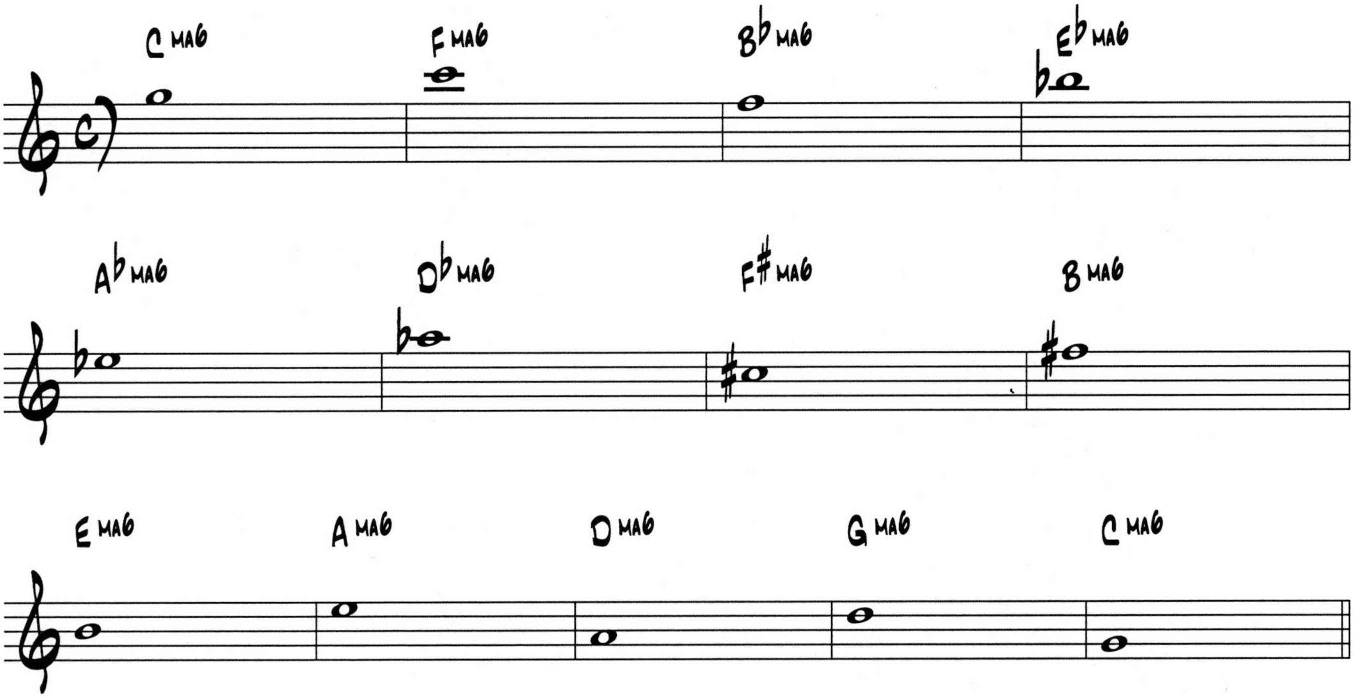

TASTING SIXTHS ON MAJOR 6TH CHORDS

TRACK 75 - BOSSA

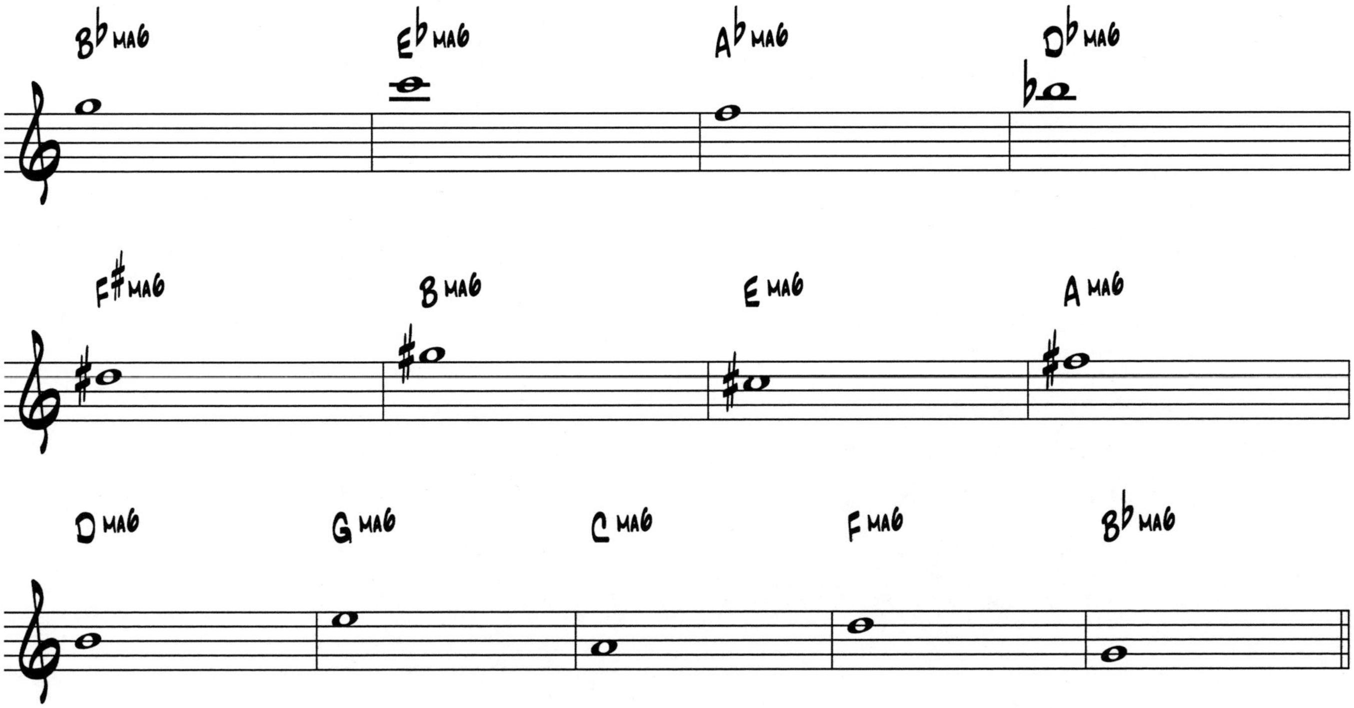

TASTING NINTHS ON MAJOR 6TH CHORDS

TRACK 76 - SAMBA

TASTING ROOTS ON MINOR 6TH CHORDS

TRACK 77 TWO-FEEL

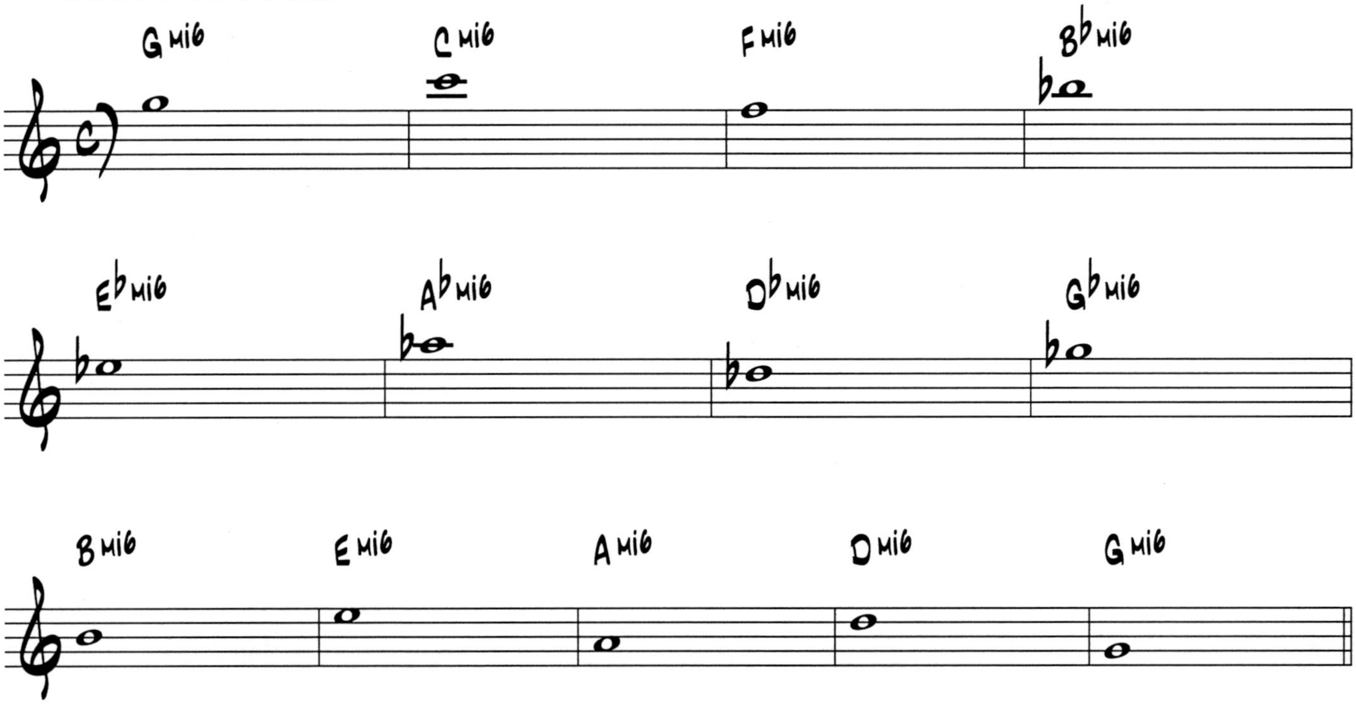

TASTING THIRDS ON MINOR 6TH CHORDS

TRACK 78 - SWING

TASTING FIFTHS ON MINOR 6TH CHORDS

TRACK 79 - BOSSA

TASTING SIXTHS ON MINOR 6TH CHORDS

TRACK 80 - BOSSA

TASTING NINTHS ON MINOR 6TH CHORDS

TRACK 81 - SWING

About the Author

Saxophonist and flutist Greg Fishman is an accomplished performer, recording artist, author, teacher and clinician. Born in Chicago in 1967, he began playing professionally at age fourteen. Greg graduated from DePaul University in Chicago with a degree in Jazz Performance, and earned a Masters Degree in Jazz Pedagogy from Northwestern University. He is among the foremost experts on the music of Stan Getz and is the author of three Getz transcription books published by Hal Leonard. His self-published books, *Jazz Saxophone Etudes, Volumes 1 – 3, Jazz Saxophone Duets*, *Volumes 1 – 3, Jazz Phrasing for Beginners, Jazz Guitar Etudes* and *Jazz Trumpet Duets* are in circulation worldwide and have been endorsed by top educators and jazz performers, including Michael Brecker, Jerry Coker and Phil Woods.

Greg is a contributing author of jazz theory articles for Jazz Improv magazine, JAZZed, Chicago Jazz Magazine, IAJE Jazz Educators Journal, and was featured on the cover of *Saxophone Journal*, for whom he also writes. He is the author of the liner notes for the Verve reissue of the Getz recording *The Steamer.*

Greg has toured and performed worldwide with his own group, and with such artists as Phil Woods, the Woody Herman Band, Louis Bellson, Slide Hampton, Conte Candoli, Lou Levy, Clark Terry, Jackie and Roy, Don Menza, Ira Sullivan, Judy Roberts, Jeremy Monteiro, Jimmy Heath, Lou Donaldson, Harry Allen, Jeff Hamilton, Eddie Higgins, and Benny Golson.

Greg is the co-founder, along with Brazilian guitarist/vocalist, Paulinho Garcia, of the award-winning duo, "Two for Brazil." They perform worldwide, and have recorded five CDs. Greg's current discography features additional jazz releases in the U.S., Singapore, and Japan.

In addition to clubs and concerts in the U.S., Greg has been featured at the Concord-Fujitsu jazz festival in Japan, the NorthSea Jazz Festival in the Netherlands, and in numerous concerts in Hong Kong, Bangkok, Singapore, China and Israel.

Greg teaches jazz master classes and college workshops nationally and internationally, and is on the faculty of the Jamey Aebersold Summer Jazz Workshop.

When not on tour, Greg is based in the Chicago area where he performs locally and teaches at Greg Fishman Jazz Studios.

Greg Fishman is a Rico artist and plays Rico reeds exclusively.

"...His solos are shrewdly conceived yet delivered with apparent ease and elegance. He develops harmonies that sometimes startle the ear as he forges lines that take unexpected twists and turns..."
— Chicago Tribune

"Greg Fishman dares to explore new musical heights. Every lesson in Greg's books is a must for all musicians, and this latest book is no exception. Greg, you've done a beautiful, musical thing again!"
— James Moody